Dove Prophecies

Prophesies, dreams and visions on how to save North America from the New World Order plan of total enslavement. The Salvation revealed requires the rejoining of the Native American priesthood with the Hebrew Melkizedek priesthood in renewing an ancient covenant existing for over 3000 years.

Abbot David Michael, ThD
info@glentivar.org
719 4231 9109

Glentivar Village Press

Preparing for more difficult times with faith, hope and love for the future.

POB 101, Buena Vista, CO. 81211
http://glentivar.org
ISBN 978-0692382837
Edition 1.4
Fully Copyright Protected
February 20, 2015

Prologue

This is perhaps the only book of its kind in this modern era that reveals what needs to be done to save what can be saved of the FREE people in America. It proposes the reviving of an ancient covenant between the Hebrew Melkizedek priesthood and the priesthood of the Native American tribes so the land might again be productive and its people have protection from enemy forces.

In suggesting the saving of the American people, I admit it will not stop a great destruction of life – as much as 70% of the American population will die. The UN/NWO forces will soon promote the invasion by millions of foreign troops, man-made natural disasters and disease pandemics.

It is not saved through trying to expose the activities of the NWO or by confronting the political and economic demigods of our time. The battle is in the heavenlies and have to do with birthrights, bloodlines and the Melkizedek priesthood as the forerunners to the emergence of the 144,000 prophets who fight the Antichrist during the 2nd half of the Great Tribulation.

For most Americans, the best solution is to disconnect from government controlled utilities and systems to then live off-grid and self-sufficiently in very remote areas. Very limited fossil fuel dependency is advised with most energy coming from renewable fuels and alternative energy. Food grown on site in the wilderness will become a must. If these veggie gardens can be made to be mobile such as on large trailers, this is even better.

The emergence of the Sisters of the Dove as reported in this book is extremely important and timely in this period of history as you will see in the chapters to follow on the Dove Prophecies.

Index

Chapter 1	Sisters of the Dove	5
Chapter 2	Life of Abbot David Michael	15
Chapter 3	Dream: Native Princess`	23
Chapter 4	Dream: Native Drums	27
Chapter 5	Dream: Chief Whitefeather	29
Chapter 6	Dream: Native Horse Woman	34
Chapter 7	Dream: Blue Angel & the 7 Doves	40
Chapter 8	Meeting the Dove Sisters	44
Chapter 9	Prophecy: Anishinabe [Anasazi] 7 Fires	51
Chapter 10	Prophecy: Blue and Red Kachina	62
Chapter 11	History: Anasazi History	69
Chapter 12	Translating the Hopi Tablets	75
Chapter 13	Prophecy: Hebrew-Native Alliance	87
Chapter 14	Dream: Curse of the Buffalo	89
Chapter 15	Dream: Ark of the Covenant	91
Chapter 16	Visitation: Army of the 4 Winds	100
Chapter 17	Vision of George Washington	106
Chapter 18	Dream: Feed the Children	114

Chapter 1: Sisters of the Dove

The information I am going to present in this chapter is very new to me. Very new as the 1st of February 2014 is when it all came together in my understanding.

I have always known that there were high ranking female angels from encounters with male angels but never really did a study on this topic and never met one.

From the testimonies of the women of the line of King David who I have been dealing with for years, a number of themes and archetypes have emerged.

The moon, the dove, the horse and the color blue are reoccurring themes. I knew there was a reason for all this but did not make the connection until recently. I did receive a hint at what I am going to share from a dream I had some time ago gthat I called the 7 sisters of Bathsheba.

Sisters Hunted by Orion

Regarding the constellation of the 7 Sisters of the Pleiades in an earlier book, I showed that this sisterhood of 7 stars is representative of a female angelic host. The female part of YHWH as created into the angelic species reflecting the male and female natures of the Godhead.

I also proposed that they are being hunted by Orion the Hunter to the West who wants to rule over them and pollute them. This hunter constellation of Orion is currently dominated by the powers of darkness and is the domain of the great dragon of the book of Revelation.

I am now of the opinion that the 7 sisters constellation is inhabited by a female dominant species that some will call angelic. In my earlier article, I showed the moon in its celestial movement assists in hiding them from the hunter.

In myth these 7 sisters are associated with the dove and the color blue. Among the Hopis, they are referred to as associated with the work of the Blue Kachina.

Gabriella Original Name

While doing a study on archangels, I discovered the Roman Church sometime in history changed the name of Gabriella to Gabriel as the name of one of the archangels. In earlier times, Gabriel was identified by the Church as a female angel and not of the male gender representation. There is some debate whether angels can really have gender but it does seem they take on the outward image of their core natures and traits. If they have predominately feminine traits, they appear to mankind as feminine. If they have masculine traits they than appear masculine. Archangel Michael is very masculine. I know this because as I have seen him personally.

It is said that Rome did this change of gender for Gabrielle because they did not want more than one female 'deity' in their paganized Christian 'Trinity' religion. Only Mary as the Mother of God was to be exulted in replacing the person of the Holy Spirit in this pagan trinity. In this pagan trinity, we have god the father, god the son as a child and the mother of god or god the mother who cares for son and rules son.

This ideal originates in the Babylonian religion where Nimrod as God died and was then incarnated into the son so the father is the son reincarnated with the goddess mother who is the Theotokos or Mother of God forming a matriarchal religion.

By the time of the rise of the Roman Empire, this belief was known as the religion of Mithra (the son) in which Constantine the Great adhered to all of this life. The son was reborn on every December 25th each year and this pagan holy day became the Christmas date for Christians around the world. Roman Pagans now calling themselves Christians conspired to change the gender identity of Gabriella (female) to Gabriel (male) to distance and subdue the true feminine nature of Gabrielle.

Patron for Female Priesthood

I am now of the thinking that Gabrielle is the female angelic patron for the female priesthood on earth as is Michael for the male priesthood. Of course Y'Shua rules over all in a supreme command status as King of Kings given to him by YHWH himself. This is because Y'Shua made the greatest sacrifice for the saving of the human soul in giving himself to the death upon the cross. In this act is Salvation offered for all who will come to the Father YHWH through Y'Shua.

I suggest Gabrielle is the patron for the Sisters of the Dove associated with the 7 sisters of the Pleiades. Gabrielle was the archangel who met with Mary and from which she conceived Jesus [Y'Shua]. This is really a woman to woman sister kind of love in fulfilling the promise of YHWH where the seed of the woman would bruise the head of the serpent (sin).

Be assured Gabrielle is NOT Ishtar. Ishtar is traced back to an Anunnaki alien royal person and was originally called Ianna in Sumeria. Ianna was later translated as Ishter (Easter), Venus and Isis. <u>Do not be deceived by this imposter goddess!</u> Ianna/Ishtar/Easter/Venus/Isis is not of angelic origin but is a lower deity species below the rank of archangel. This entity is claiming to be a god in association with the Anunnaki royal house of RA who now rules over the empire of Nibiru and claims to be the creator of mankind.

Blue Kachina

The connection of blue to the nature of Gabrielle is cross-cultural. Throughout history, blue is the color of the Hebrew priesthood whereas red is the color of the Roman 'antichrist' priesthood. I once wore red robes as a bishop in the Roman Catholic Church of the East called Orthodox. I have since repented and now blue is a color of choice for me as a bishop and abbot.

Tara Greene who is a psychic has much of what she understands to be right and had this to say about this topic.

> *"The Star Bird has been prophesied by various cultures, the Hopi, Mayan and others. This is the Blue Kachina of the Hopis. The Star Bird as a dove is similar to the dove always depicted with the Archangel Gabriel[le] symbolizing the Holy Spirit. All Renaissance paintings of the Annunciation show the Holy Dove descending from heaven on a ray of golden or white light."*

The Hopi connection to the blue dove is very significant and will become a major door for a solution for them in the near future in finally entering into the 7th Fire of the Ojibwe Prophesies that I discuss later in this book.

Citing the most ancient reference to Gabriella, we find her job description from chapter 20 in the Book of Enoch. The book of Enoch was written before the great flood of Noah's time and may only be surpassed as the most ancient book of the bible by the book of Job.

When the flood came, Enoch was taken up to heaven and did not die. It is said Enoch was one of the last humans to live extensively among the angels rather than among mankind.

Chapter 20:
Saraqael(7) one of the holy angels, who is set over the spirits, who sin in the spirit.
<u>Gabriel, one of the holy (8) angels, who is over Paradise and the serpents [seraphims] and the Cherubim.</u>

Remiel, one of the holy angels, whom God set over those who rise.

In this most ancient job description we find Archangel Gabriella having the oversight over three areas in the vast Kingdom of YHWH. She had oversight over Paradise as to who would be there or not be there. Of course, Paradise may still exist but now the faithful have direct access to heaven as a result of the shed blood sacrifice of Y'Shua on the cross.

Her angelic power over serpents or the seraphim connects back to Eve when it was promised by YHWH that her seed would bruise the head of the serpent and from her seed the serpent would be overcome. This angelic power to overcome serpents now empowers the genetic line of Eve to be vindicated for being deceived by the Serpent in the Garden of Eden earlier named Sama-el that is also called Satan and in the book of Revelation, the great dragon.

This promise has been passed down through the female line of Eve from the time of the fall of mankind when sin or rebellion against YHWH entered into the world among the Edenic humans. From this emerges the Melkizedek priesthood for women that I call the the Sisters of the Dove.

I will say not all humans living today stem directly from the Adam and Eve of the Garden of Eden. However, most now through human species intermarriage have a genetic link to this common origin.

Having responsibility for the Cherubim is noteworthy. The Cherubim surrounded the throne of YHWH and gave him worship day and night. Gabrielle as female in nature is a worshiper of YHWH in a manner that a man cannot worship. As a female who is able to give herself to a man, so is she able to give herself to God in a pure worship where she can become fully encompassed in God's embrace.

Abbot David Michael

From **KimbasAngels.com** we are given a historical religious overview of who Gabriella is in her nature as she continued with her heavenly and earthly responsibilities. Much of the quote to follow is what man has traditionally attributed as tasks for Gabriella and are not necessarily what she actually does. I include this here for reference.

"Gabriel/Gabriella means "God is my strength" Variations of his name include: Gavriel and Gabriella. In Jewish legend/lore, Gabriel is female known as Gabriella - being the only female Archangel.

In Islamic Gabriel translates to Jibril and it is Jibril who revealed the Koran to Muhammad. She presides over Paradise, and although she is the ruling prince[ss] of the 1st heaven, she is said to sit on the left-hand side of God. Gabriel is known as the archangel of revelation, creativity, and faith."

"Apart from Michael, she is the only angel mentioned by name in the Old Testament - unless we include among the Old Testament books the Book of Tobit, usually considered apocryphal, in which case Raphael, who appears there, becomes the 3rd-named angel..."

Gabriel[le] is called the bringer of good news for throughout much of the scriptures and ancient texts she has been known to bring tidings of joy and happiness. She also helps those with talents in art and communication. "During the middle ages, Christians believed her to be the angel of light."

"Many titles have been bestowed (accredited) to Gabriel[la] through many different sources, these include; Ruler of the Sixth Heaven, Chief Ambassador to Humanity, Chief Ambassador to God, Ruling Prince[ss] of the Cherubim.

In addition, names such as Divine Herald, Angel of Revelation, Angel of Aspirations, Angel of Truth, Divine Female, Prince[ss] of Justice, Angel of Joy, Angel of Childbirth, Archangel of the Holy Sefiroth, Trumpeter of the Last Judgment, Governor of Eden, Angel of Vengeance, Angel of Death, Angel of Mercy, Angel of Judgment, and Angel of the Apple Tree."

"Archangel to those born under the sign: Aquarius - Pisces - Scorpio (Alternate Resources State: Pisces, Cancer, and Scorpio). [S]he is of the four winds, her direction is from the west. Being "nature-like", her energy color is blue-green. Her element is Water. Her season is winter. Tree: Willow (Though she is also Angel of the Apple Tree - conflicting sources). Her symbol is that of a trumpet. Colors representative: white and silver."

Blows the Last Trumpet

One of the upcoming tasks for Gabriella is the blowing of the last trumpet revealed in the books of Isaiah and Revelations. In this we find YHWH as the Creator of Creators has chosen an archangel of female qualities to bring in the end of this age.

It is the final trumpet 'nail' that overcomes the serpent Satan also known as the great dragon as promised would happen to Eve by YHWH. She blows the 'last trumpet' that brings a final end to the rule of deception of the serpent in the cosmos. This is a clear picture of the female 'getting back' at Satan for being deceived by Satan in the Garden.

Lucifer/Sama-el or Satan is of the class of Seraphim – one step above the archangels in angelic species and power. Serif means serpent. It follows Lucifer is serpentine or dragon-like in his ethereal body. This then is where the female nature of YHWH in created woman finally overcomes Lucifer, that rebellious angelic seraphim, and all he has gathered behind him in the great war against YHWH.

Angel of the Moon and Dreams

Another source tells us that Gabriella is identified as the Angel of the Moon and an angel of the 1st Heaven. Gabriel transmits God's messages to mankind. Angel of the Altitudes and Angel of Annunciation. The Angel of Aspirations and Dreams. According to the Jewish cabala, the Moon is the angel of aspirations and dreams in occult lore and this is the angel Gabriella. She is one of the angels of creation and the angel of dreams.

I am not really wanting to give credit to occult sources when citing these sources yet it does align itself with what I have discovered about Gabrielle from my experiences and other biblical and extrabiblical studies.

Male/Female Guarding the Ark

It is from the male/female Creator duality that I am now understanding that even the Ark of the Covenant is portrayed as both male and female. The two angels that were placed by Moses over the Ark of the Covenant I now believe to represent the archangel's Michael (masculine nature) and Gabrielle (feminine nature) as the angelic Merkaba of YHWH.

There are many societies among the occult world who have embraced the male/female duality of god but we need to understand that angelic or aliens species ARE NOT gods and should NEVER be worshipped.

There is but one God of both male and female natures and his/her name is YHWH yet in this even his name represents a masculine/feminine duality. YHWH or YaHuVeHa or even when written backwards as 'Hayah Havah' literally means "He who originates all things (male- seed) – She who nurtures all things (female - womb)."

The merkaba is the joining of the two natures of male and female to represent the creator in his/her duality as a single entity. It is the three dimensional star of David that historically has represented this duality. I have observed an actual rock crystal in my dreams of this shape having infinite power so it is more than just a metaphoric symbol. It is also found in supra-nature.

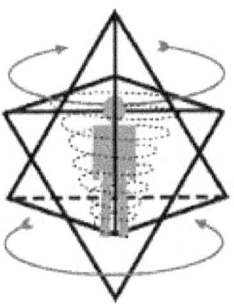

The upper three-sided pyramid pointing to heaven is the male component that counter rotates with the female lower three-sided pyramid that points to earth. This creates an energy vortex between heaven and earth that can link the powers of heaven to earth that the earth may align itself with the frequencies of heaven where YHWH dwells. It is then true that what happens in heaven then will then happen on earth as the male/female natures of God join as one in human form.

What is Emerging?

I have attempted to show that there is a feminine natured archangel in history and theology and that this same archangel Gabrielle is to blow the last trumpet to overcome the rule of the serpent in bringing in the end of the age. I have come to realise Gabrielle is the natural patron choice for the 7 sisters of the Pleiades, is to be considered the blue dove angel, is of the royal-priestly colour of blue and is connected with the coming of the blue Kachina to the Hopis.

This female priesthood is the female complement of the Order of Melkizedek. I am calling them the "Sisters of the Dove" since this is a reoccurring theme and image among those of this calling. This membership is a calling from above and cannot be bestowed onto another by man or woman but is a calling by YHWH alone.

It is genetic in that those who are so called will likely have a genetic bloodline to the royal line of King David and to Bathsheba. The name Bathsheba also means the daughters or sisters associated with the dove.

I believe it is from this female order that a new king-priest royal line will emerge for the Millennium (1000 years) to rule with Y'Shua upon the earth. More on this in a later writing.

My role in all this as a Melchizedek priest is to protect the Sisters of the Dove from destruction so they may fulfil their mission in these last days. I am being called to them as a father-priest or in some cases like a husband-priest to guide them to assure they do not falter from their calling. One of the Sisters has given me the name of Dovekeeper which I like the best.

I have so far met 5 woman who have been called by YHWH to this Order. I do not yet know if these 5 will all survive the difficulty in preparing for this mission against the great dragon. I must acknowledge what the scriptures tell us, "Many are called but few are chosen."

This sadly tells us many are given the mission as one of the Sisters of the Dove but only a few will manage to prayerfully give themselves to a state of purity sufficiently to be able to fulfil this very specialised 'royal' mission. Keep the Sisters of the Dove in your prayers.

Chapter 2: Life of David Michael

A prophet was I called,
on Mt Zion at age 12.
With music as my sword,
and faith as my shield.

I lived in frontier Oregon,
and cared for horse and cow.
Spent many nights a sleeping,
by the stream and on the mount.

In school I was most brazen,
yet to college I was sent.
Excelled with degrees a-plenty,
then a professor for 20 years spent.

Ordained a Deacon cleric,
in the Syro-Chaldean faith,
Then ordained an Episcopal Priest,
a chaplain to serve the American Way.

Then received the mantle of Bishop,
in the Orthodox domain.
These accolades I count as a beginning,
to now seek the more Holy Way.

Rejected by carnal fathers and
banned from the synod of Bishops.
My words cut too deep I was told
Now to exile I have been driven.

At 10,000 feet I lived for years,
to the high Rockies I did turn.
As a prophet I did begin,
To a prophet I must now return.

Abbot David Michael

With llamas in the high mountains,
making harps and knives my trade.
To the Native and the angel,
a 'windwalker' some they say.

Glentivar now my home of training,
In the land of Anasazi fame.
Here I sit near heaven's gate,
to learn with unbending faith.

Others may come and join me,
in this prophet and angel place.
Come ready to live in freedom,
in the wilderness, a test of faith.

Bring your tipis, tents and trailers,
to Glentivar's native land.
And hear the voice of Creator,
tell us of His awesome plan.

Into the mountains is our spirit-quest,
to find our call most dear .
Seeing angels and aliens forces,
will sharpen your warrior soul.

The mantle I wear for mountain stays,
to dwell in sacred grottoes of praise.
The birds they sing the songs I play,
as God meets me there each day.

Llamas up granite peaks I chase ,
the mountains they call them there.
I slowly climb - a shepherds fate,
and bring them home to stay.

Now living more as a pilgrim race,
freed from Mammon's binding chains.
I seek only to be in Creator's place,

to live and serve his way.

Breaking the bonds of Catholic strife,
to embrace the loving Jesus faith.
Now I live a simpler life,
the one Creator gave.

So come you weary pilgrim,
to the land above the mist.
My heart is ever seeking love,
so as to embrace you with a kiss.

My Beginnings

At the age of 5 I knew I was not like other people. I saw angels and demons all the time. I could hear spiritual forces talking to me. I could sense the angelic entities in the forces of nature like the wind, the waves of the sea, the rain and thunder. At the age of 12, I had an experience with the Holy Spirit where I spoke in other languages I did not learn.

At age 13, I went upon Mt Zion in Oregon for three days fasting and met YHWH and was given a gift in music. This was my bar misvah. I later sang in unknown languages accompanied in harmony by 3 male angels. While still in my teens, I would camp at night on the Hawaiian Heiau's (ancient stone temple mounts) in Hawaii where I then lived and sing of the power of YHWH to the spirit-gods of Hawaii. I was observed to sing in a dialect of ancient Hawaiian as confirmed by Hawaiian speakers. Hawaiians knew and the spirits knew what I was singing yet I often did not know although I did sense the meaning.

My communion with the spirit world made my ability to relate to the common natural world difficult. Although I had an open communication with native Hawaiian spirits, I did not know my future was to be in North America and communicate with the Native American spiritual world. My first sense of this destiny came as a voice to me in 2008.

Native American Origin

As I was beginning to fall asleep and praying on the 1st of March 2008, , I heard the words, "You are Native American." Immediately after hearing these words, I saw the word 'Ojibwe' in bold letters in my vision.

I cannot confirm the validity of the facts of this vision. I had been studying the history of the Native American people for the last few weeks so this was a topic in question. My dad has often told me many times he thinks we are part Native American but I have found little conclusive evidence for such.

It may be there was a blood covenant that makes me a part of the Ojibwe tribe. My dad's family has been in the Americas since the 1640's first in Massachusetts and then New York where the Ojibwe lived. My mother's side also began in NY in the mid 1600's. I have discovered they are closely related as 'white' cousins by intermarriage to the Native Mohawk families of Ransom and Tarbell dating to the early 1800's. I have recently met these Mohawk cousins.

If true, such a uniting with my Native people would represent a pre-existing 'blood' covenant between the Hebrew-Celt (my dominant origin) and the Native American as mandated in the 10 February 2008 prophecy that I will share later in this book.

Windwalker Name Given

Sometime in the night in December 2007, I was greatly disturbed as I slept and then was partially awakened and found myself hovering above the Canada - US border near Montana looking down upon the border. I was astonished to be called 'Windwalker' in this encounter by my spirit hosts who were angels. As the facts of a pending invasion on US soil were being revealed, I was still drawn to my name. I believe this prophecy is soon to be fulfilled. The number of troops involved in this invasion was staggering you you will witness in the following dream.

As I looked down at the border (about mid-US on the map) a word was spoken to me by the angel that there are 600,000 (yes - six hundred thousand) NWO-UN forces at the Border that will be ready to invade the U.S. when the time comes. As I looked closely at the invaders I saw that they were mostly Chinese military forces in the dream.

Then I saw multiple tunnels underground along the Border of Montana that penetrated deep into US territory as hidden underground highways as far south as Wyoming to be used for the invasion. I strongly understood the invasion was imminent and the time table for the invasion was moved-up (sooner) than what was previously planned due to some international incident that will soon be revealed by the media.

I was greatly disturbed by this in my Spirit. I then was fully awakened. More on this vision can be found in book 1 of the NWO series titled 2015 Alien Invasion.

Melkizedek Priest Only

More recently I have been told by YHWH that I may only be associated with the Order of Melkizedek priesthood which cannot be transferred by human ritual or events. It is solely an act of YHWH that brings one into this calling and mission as a prophet. After this divine directive, I did resign as an Orthodox-Catholic Bishop of an American Orthodox jurisdiction. I later resigned in serving as Moderator on an internet site for 19 Orthodox and Catholic denominations called FOCUS.

Since then, I have chosen to be listed and serve as Celtic-Chaldean or Culdee which is really the Order of Melkizedek among the Celts of Britain. More on this in book 4 of the NWO series called 2015 Melkizedek Arises.

What was important in this encounter is that I was called 'Windwalker' by the hosting angels which is normally a name reserved for Native Americans. I realized that this name fits me. "One who walks upon the wind" is what I do as I continue to encounter angels who under Michael the Archangel have the power of the winds as a force of justice. I do reveal more about these wind warrior angels in chapter 16 of this book.

My time with the 4th dimensional world has so changed the way I think and view reality that I can no longer fall back into the social norms and expectations of this 3rd dimensional world and modern society. I have become a social misfit and an outcast in many social circles including with my own family and five children.

I was once a college professor yet now if I returned to the halls of academia, I would be cast out as crazy. I am sometimes not aware if I am in the 4th dimensional world or the 3rd dimensional world. Only with others who also spend their time in realms not seen in the natural do I find true friendship and companionship.

Visited by the Native Elders

I have been in contact with Native American elders who have died (spirit beings) several times in my recent history which I will talk about later in this book. I do not claim to be right in all the analysis of my dreams but what I do share is my best understanding so far. I am a student and and seeker – not a master of anything. I will always choose to be the student so I might learn from others and remain teachable.

My first encounter with the counsel of the 'departed' Native American Elders was in March 2008 where we beat drums together where our hearts began to beat as one. We were in unity of the same Spirit on the same mission in this encounter.

The 2nd encounter occurred as I was told by YHWH in 2012 to search out a Chief White Feather who would in the search lead me to the right spiritual entities and the truths needed to understand the path I was to take.

On the 10th of February 2013 I had my 3rd encounter. I was told that there is a unity that will come between a small group of the white man and the Natives in fulfillment of the many prophecies. This encounter is provided later in this book.

Most recently as the 4th encounter, I met the Native counsel in the dream of the 'horse woman' found in chapter 6 of this book on the 21st of February in 2013. In this encounter, the Elders were there with Chief Whitefeather being present among them. I was given a horse as assisted by the Empress of the Holy Roman Empire who I personally know. Why she needed to assist in this I do not know. Her presence seemed out of place to me at the time.

I accepted the gift of the horse and as I took the reins, there was a native woman who popped out from under the neck of the horse and matter of factually said, "I come with the horse." She represented the Sisters of the Dove as the one I am to love in the rejoining the covenant.

She is tasked to lead her people back to the God YHWH (YaHuVeHa) of their forefathers and from this reconciliation, the barren lands of the Native Americans will be healed with rain as the return of the blue Kachina enabling the crops to again grow in abundance in the dry places.

As of the writing of this book, I am watching as the Sisters of the Dove reveal themselves to me and then come together to assure the foundations are in place to be overcomers in this war against the rebellion of the Serif Lucifer also known as Satan.

Chapter 3: Native Princess

I was 23 years old when I first saw a Native American 'princes' in my dreams. I know there are not 'princesses' in Native tribal tradition but this is what I saw in the dream. I had just married a Scottish lassie and found that her parents controlled her life in a family cult they claimed was Christian. I struggled in this relationship for 11 months wanting to survive as a free-willed human being. Sadly, my then wife was forced by her mother to choose between me and them. She finally did choose. She left me to remain with them.

During this very difficult time, I would wander the Scottish hills near Lockerbie, Scotland and pray and sing praises to YHWH seeking deliverance from this oppression. I then had a dream where I found myself on a vast prairie and I was holding a Native American woman in my arms and cradled her head in my lap. She was known to me as being a princess among her people. She seemed to be dying and I sensed in the dream I was supposed to revive her. I held her very lovingly and prayed that YHWH would give this Native princess life to live and not die. She then seemed to be more rested and not as tense. It seemed the threat of death had left her.

I later shared this dream with my then wife's parents and they told me if I had the dream again, I was to kill her in the dream. They had already had me burn my Thompson chain reference bible I cherished since I used it to confront them. I had the dream again the next night but I could not bring myself to kill her but wanted her to live.

The fact is I loved her – a woman I had never met or seen. What was most memorable to me was the way she looked at me with the eyes of "please save me" as I held her head in my lap in protecting her from evil and death. I now know she represented the tragedy of the Native American peoples.

I never did tell the now ex-inlaws of what I had done in having her live and not die. I know they thought I had killed her in the dream. I think I may have lied to them saying she was dead to save her from them. No more was said of this.

For may years to come I wondered who this woman was. After another failed marriage, I prayed again and asked YHWH why I had been so messed up in choosing the right woman he had for me in ministry and in life. I came to realize I am not to be married in the normal sense but be in companionship because of a higher mission in the Kingdom of YHWH. Traditional marriage was not to be for me.

I have yet to discover the Native woman, if she is a real person, as the one who will emerge from the gathering of the Sisters of the Dove. With one of the sisters of the Dove, I went through some very difficult times with in trying to discover if she was the one of my dreams. I wondered if she was the right one.

I then received this email from David Scott Shute who is a claimed prophet with some credibility.

> "I was just laying here listening to the Book Of Enoch audio and while praying in the Spirit I was given a vision. In the vision I saw you sitting somewhere outside it seems and your lady was <u>laying with her head on your lap</u>.

I knew she was divine sent to you 100% guaranteed this is truth. I saw she was the supply the Lord had prepared for you to assist you in your work.

He [God] spoke to me and said he was pleased with you and your worship is as precious to Him as David's was. He told me that most supposed worship was disgusting and not worth Him listening to. He said you were one of the few that had His ear. I pray this is encouragement to you.

Then he told me to ask you to worship Him and direct it towards me and that if you do He will answer the prayers I have asked him regarding my healing which I have never received. He said if you will worship Him and direct it towards me I would receive all He has reserved for me to experience.

What struck me in this prophecy is the fact I was holding this native woman with her head cradled in my lap in the vision of David Shute the same way I first saw her over 35 years ago. David Shute did not know this fact. She was in reality just age 8 at the time of my early dream of her so her calling was already known. This vision stopped me from walking away from her at the time.

Then I had this dream of holding this Native woman on my lap <u>again</u> on the 21st of January 2014. In this dream the woman was clearly the woman I was wondering about who I first met when selling the sacred land of Glentivar to her parents.

It was at Glentivar that most of my dreams have come to me over the past 5 years. Glentivar I have been told is the "land of angels and prophets." Many who came there have seen angels or heard them speaking to them.

My future seems to be set. I just need to relax and let God be God. Sadly this women has left the Sisters of the Dove so I do not know how YHWH will make all this happen. Will she return when the time is right? I do not know. Will YHWH raise up another Native woman who will take her place in this mission? I do not know.

I do know I need to lay down my life in loving all around me and the Sisters of the Dove and be there for them, protect them and assist their mission on this earth under the Kingship of Y'Shua with the help of Michael and Gabrielle as the male and female complement of the Order of Melkizedek.

Chapter 4: Dream- Native Drums

In the early morning of the 11th of march 2008, I had a dream-vision where I found myself among a small group of people around a camp fire. I noticed most were Native Americans. It was late at night and the fire lit up the faces of the men and woman in the circle but not much else was visible.

As we all sat and began drumming together, the beat of the drums aligned with the beat of our human hearts and all of the hearts who had gathered together around the fire began to beat their drums together as one heart and we sang as one voice in worship to Creator. This one heartbeat of the group began to allow telepathic communications between all who had gather in the drumming circle. We were enabled to know what was the mission for each one there in the group so the mission never needed to be spoken out loud.

The group of men and woman are perhaps related to the 70 prophets from another dream in book 1 except this group were associated with the Native American people.

It is well documented that the Federalists and NWO factions within the US Government have acted upon a plan of of both secret and open genocide of Native Americans for hundreds of years.

Such activities include starvation, economic dependency, forced sterilization, the release of deadly diseases and toxic 'energy' onto tribal lands and the stealing of the better land that can produce food and income.

In opposing these evil forces, the only survival of the tribal people will come through a tribal unity where Y'Shua will lead them into a full self-reliance and independence from Federalist controls, their subsidies and the intrusive government and NWO backed religious organizations.

This does not mean war is imminent but it does suggest the mission is more likely a move toward a complete self-sufficiency from the resources found on the land rather than a continued reliance on Federal government subsidies.

I would suggest that any direct confrontation with US Federalist police or military forces would be disastrous at this time. Alternately, the need is to develop existing natural resources with innovative designs to become completely independent and to become more covert by living in more hidden places. I believe such designs will come by revelation from the Holy Spirit.

As to the details of this covert mission...it remains a secret and is revealed to those that are led by the Holy Spirit to the campfire 'pow- wow' with drums in hand at the appointed time.

Chapter 5: Dream-Vision
In search of Chief White Feather

The Dream

As I slept in on November 10th 2012, I had a dream where I saw a picture of an old Native American man and underneath the picture was his name. The name was "Chief White Feather" etched on a brass plaque. The picture seemed like an old black and white photograph of the 19th century.

What I did notice was the feather. It was white but at the base of the feather it was very fluffy. My sense in the dream is that I was to find this man and he would have the revelation that I needed to know and understand.

I did a search on the name Chief White Feather and initially found a Native man of the Sioux that was a Christian evangelist. Not seeing a spiritual connection, I continued the search and found another Chief Whitefeather from among the Hopi tribe in Arizona. He had shared an ancient prophecy about the coming of the Pahana which is the Hopi name for Messiah. I intuitively knew this was the right man.

Abbot David Michael

The following Hopi prophecy that I needed to understand is included here and was shared by Chief Whitefeather of the Hopi Bear Clan to a christian minister in about 1958. I was convinced this was the right chief as it dealt with the Anasazi and the descendant Hopi tribes that I was studying and seeking the spiritual key to understand this culture and their importance to the future survival of the people of North America. The story of the prophecy is as follows.

The Prophecy

This extraordinary Hopi prophecy was first published in a mimeographed manuscript that circulated among several Methodist and Presbyterian churches in 1959. Some of the prophecies were published in 1963 by Frank Waters in The Book of the Hopi.

The account begins by describing how, while driving along a desert highway one hot day in the summer of 1958, a minister named David Young stopped to offer a ride to an Indian elder, who accepted with a nod. After riding in silence for several minutes, the Indian said:

"I am White Feather, a Hopi of the ancient Bear Clan. In my long life I have traveled through this land, seeking out my brothers, and learning from them many things full of wisdom. I have followed the sacred paths of my people, who inhabit the forests and many lakes in the east, the land of ice and long nights in the north, and the places of holy altars of stone built many years ago by my brothers' fathers in the south. From all these I have heard the stories of the past, and the prophecies of the future.

Today, many of the prophecies have turned to stories, and few are left -- the past grows longer, and the future grows shorter.

"And now White Feather is dying. His sons have all joined his ancestors, and soon he too shall be with them. But there is no one left, no one to recite and pass on the ancient wisdom. My people have tired of the old ways -- the great ceremonies that tell of our origins, of our emergence into the Fourth World, are almost all abandoned, forgotten, yet even this has been foretold. The time grows short.

"My people await Pahana, the lost White Brother, as do all our brothers in the land. He will not be like the white men we know now, who are cruel and greedy. We were told of their coming long ago. But still we await Pahana.

"He will bring with him the symbols, and the missing piece (broken corner) of that sacred tablet now kept by the elders, given to him when he left, that shall identify him as our True White Brother.

"The Fourth World shall end soon, and the Fifth World will begin. This the elders everywhere know. The Signs over many years have been fulfilled, and so few are left.

"This is the First Sign: We are told of the coming of the white-skinned men, like Pahana, but not living like Pahana men who took the land that was not theirs. And men who struck their enemies with thunder.

"This is the Second Sign: Our lands will see the coming of spinning wheels filled with voices. In his youth, my father saw this prophecy come true with his eyes -- the white men bringing their families in wagons across the prairies."

"This is the Third Sign: A strange beast like a buffalo but with great long horns, will overrun the land in large numbers. These White Feather saw with his eyes -- the coming of the white man's cattle."

"This is the Fourth Sign: The land will be crossed by snakes of iron."

"This is the Fifth Sign: The land shall be crisscrossed by a giant spider's web."

"This is the Sixth sign: The land shall be crisscrossed with rivers of stone that make pictures in the sun."

"This is the Seventh Sign: You will hear of the sea turning black, and many living things dying because of it."

"This is the Eight Sign: You will see many youth, who wear their hair long like my people, come and join the tribal nations, to learn their ways and wisdom."

"And this is the Ninth and Last Sign: You will hear of a dwelling-place in the heavens, above the earth, that shall fall with a great crash. It will appear as a blue star. Very soon after this, the ceremonies of my people will cease."

"These are the Signs that great destruction is coming. The world shall rock to and fro. The white man will battle against other people in other lands -- with those who possessed the first light of wisdom. There will be many columns of smoke and fire such as White Feather has seen the white man make in the deserts not far from here."

"Only those which come will cause disease and a great dying. Many of my people, understanding the prophecies, shall be safe. Those who stay and live in the places of my people also shall be safe. Then there will be much to rebuild. And soon -- very soon afterward -- Pahana will return. He shall bring with him the dawn of the Fifth World. He shall plant the seeds of his wisdom in their hearts. Even now the seeds are being planted. These shall smooth the way to the Emergence into the Fifth World."

"But White Feather shall not see it. I am old and dying. You -- perhaps will see it. In time, in time..."

The old Indian fell silent. They had arrived at his destination, and Reverend David Young stopped to let him out of the car. They never met again. Reverend Young died in 1976, so he did not live to see the further fulfillment of this remarkable prophecy.

Thoughts

This prophecy when considered with the Ojibwe prophecy of the 7 fires tells a story of the future and provides a context for the past. It tells of the joining of the white man and the Native in a unity that will allow the land to become fertile once again and provide for the new nation that will arise from this fusion of races.

Chapter 6: Dream- Native Horse Woman

The Dream

In the early morning of the 21st of February 2013, I had a dream about the Native Americans and their return to the God YHWH (YaHuVeHa) of their forefathers.

In the dream I was approached by Lynda Von Habsburg, the Empress of the Holy Roman Empire and told I was given a horse by the Native American Elders. I could see behind her a group of Native Americans who appeared to be Elders of the Native peoples who had 'passed on' and were in allegiance with YHWH. My sense is they were representing all of the native tribes in North America and not just one tribe. I do remember chief Whitefeather who I saw in another dream standing among them so he was counted among the Native Elders of YHWH.

A little distance away stood before me a mare of sorrel color and of very good confirmation. This was the horse I was to be given by the Native Elders. I approached the horse and began to stroke its neck and talk to the mare in comforting tones. Suddenly appearing under the neck of the horse was a beautiful Native American woman who was holding the reins. She looked at me and said very matter of factually and without hesitation, "I come with the horse."

Horse Becomes a Woman

Strangely, I immediately began speaking to the native woman as if she was the horse. I do not know why I did this but I did this all through this dream.

I thought to myself, "If she is my horse, I will not be able to ride her to get around. She is much too fragile." There was no sexual connotation to this since I was treating her now as the horse I was given.

As the Native woman came into the foreground, the horse and woman seemed to merge into one with the Native woman remaining as the one person of the two. The others in the dream began to fad into the background except for some older native mothers who remained in the background. These older women now stood about 5 paces behind the Native woman who became one with the horse. We were now alone.

We began to walk together. She was a very beautiful Native woman wearing a light colored deer skin dress. Her legs were long and slender of a most beautiful form. She wore very high heels with the toe of the heel making the shape of a horses hoof around her toes which I could see. Her toes showed through the front of the shoes and had bright red nail polish.

I asked her, "Is it difficult to walk on just two legs instead of four?" still treating her as if she was the horse given to me. She said, "It was difficult at first but not now."

As we continued to walk, I asked about the origin of her tribe and nation. I asked her if she was Pinto, Mustang - still treating her as if she were the horse and a horse breed as her tribe. She just looked at me and smiled.

Stream Begins to Flow

We walked from a higher place down in elevation and were now walking in a shallow gully that was dry. As we entered the dry stream bed having conversation, water slowly began to flow from behind us and rise up over our feet as we walked. Just a very small trickle at first then it widened and the current became much swifter but never more than 4" deep as we walked on sand and small pebbles below our feet under the water.

As we were walking down stream, I heard something behind me. I turned and saw a large group of older Native American women following us and listening into our conversation. I asked the horse woman about them and she said they always follow her.

I then tenderly took her hand in mine as we continued to walk down stream. I intuitively knew she would be there beside me as a committed friend and companion. Yes the same woman of a dream that I had received over 25 years earlier. I knew she would follow me where ever I would go.

This bond I sensed in the dream was more than a just a deep friendship but I had a sense it was a divine covenant made in heaven among the Elders in the renewing of a promise that had long since been forgotten. A covenant between the Hebrew tribes of Israel and the Native tribes of America.

Interpretation

I believe the woman and the horse are the same person. I am persuaded the horse woman has 'horse' in her name or the symbol of a horse in her family or is closely associated with the horse in her culture – so much so she is identified as being a horse among her own native people – perhaps of a horse clan.

The women who followed behind us are the matriarchal leaders of their Native tribal clans. They were watching her to identify the 'persons' of covenant for their people. Both Lynda and chief Whitefeather were in the dream who I recognized but no one else. I understood the horse woman to be the woman who would show the way for the rebirth of the YHWH (YaHuVeHa) Covenant between a line of the ancient Hebrew priesthood and the priesthood of the Native American.

I was also shown after the dream something about the water that began to flow. This represented the mission of the Blue Kachina in bringing life back to the land with the coming of life-giving water. Only after we were together in the unity of love did the water begin to flow. With the holding of our hands together, this represented the return of the Native people back to YaHuWeHa, the God of their forgathers and to the Anasazi Covenant that existed between 800 and 1200 AD as the 4th fire of the Ojibwe 7 Fires prophecies.

The return to this ancient covenant will bring with it life with the coming of rain back to the lands of the Native American in certain sacred areas. The four winds under the command of the Archangel Michael will bring these waters to the dry lands of promise and covenant. It will also provide for the protection of all those living among the Native Americans who have returned to the faith and practice of YHWH as Hebrew Christians. This is perhaps the beginning of the 7th Fire of the Ojibwe prophecies.

Native Women Take the Lead

What is implied in that only Native Woman were following us in the stream is it will be the Native Woman of the various Native tribes and clans that will take the lead in bringing their people back to YHWH in worship. When the covenant is renewed, YHWH will look from heaven and heal their land.

II Chronicles 7:14 is the scripture I was given following this dream. It reads:

> **"If my people which are called by my name, shall humble themselves, and pray, and seek my face,and turn from their wicked ways; The will I hear from heaven, and forgive their sin, and will heal their land."**

As the text from Chronicles declares to us, we must first, 1) Choose to listen to YHWH, 2) Hear what he is saying to us, 3) repent from our rebellion against him and , 4) Turn from our wicked ways. When we take these steps, then 5) YHWH will come to the land with nurturing water that brings life to the land and to its people and heal it.

I am led by the Holy Spirit to understand the 4 winds will be assigned to drive the needed rains into the 4-corners area and other sacred areas of America in bringing much needed water for agriculture. This promise is the biblical proof of the promise of the Blue Kachina that the Native lands will be healed and crops will again grow in abundance.

Chapter 7: Dream – Blue Angel, Seven 'Dove' Sisters & Bathsheba

The Dream

As I slept on the night of January 2012, I was awakened in the middle of the night with the words, "Seven sisters of the moon" as it wrote itself across my mind.

This sparked a search on the life of Bathsheba (bat Sheba) meaning 'daughter of the oath' or 'daughter of Sheba'. The Kingdom of Sheba included part of Egypt at the time of Bathsheba and King David in about 1000 BC according to Josephus.

Queen(s) of Sheba

At that time, Sheba and Egypt were united so the Queen of Sheba that met with Solomon some years later was a queen of both a part of the Sinai and also Egypt during a time when the Amun priests were ruling as pharaohs in upper Egypt.

The name suggests that Bathsheba may have had a family connection to the royal house of Sheba and the pharaohs of the past. Since Bathsheba was the mother of Solomon, to pursue her is to pursue the royal line of King David and Solomon.

After the dream and more research, I discovered that Bathsheba also literally means 'daughter of [the] seven' thought to be a name given to her in honor of the Pleiades representing the seven 'goddesses' or angels favored in North Syria. As such, the name further makes a compelling connection with Sheba and Egypt.

Some spiritualists today associate the seven sisters with the seven Chakras of the body as internal 'star-gates' of passage for the reactivation of our original DNA. I am not sure what to think about this.

Orion in the Chase

In the morning, I continued the search on the topic and found that the stars of the Seven Sisters are located just to the right of the Orion belt of the Pleiades constellation (below but off the picture) and it is currently 'hiding' behind the moon as viewed from S. Africa.

The legend is the hunter Orion (now under Draconian alien control) is in the chase of the Seven Sisters in a hunt and has found the Seven Sisters now hiding behind the moon as a strategy for escape. The seven sisters are often referred to as seven doves in this context suggesting a gentle approach to life. The 7 daughters in this context also represent the 7 churches in Revelation.

Chi Rho

In other writings, I have identified the Pleiades as originally the Chi-Rho as used to represent Christ whereas Orion appears in other sources to also be a rival 'god' that seeks to overcome the Seven Sisters to have the rule over them and pollute them.

It is the moon that provides refuge for the seven doves who are 'flying' close to the Pleiades. This may all seem fantasy but it was the words I received being awakened from sleep. I can only say it has spiritual importance for what is occurring in this time.

Chinese Festival

The Chinese have held a 'festival of the seven sisters' over the last 1500 years that is a time when a young woman seeks a suitable mate. This suggests it is a time when good occurs and a life of peace is assured when the doves of the seven sisters seek and find true love.

Amun-Ra

The Egyptian god prominent during the time of 1000 BC was Amun-Ra which may be associated with Orion in this context and was one of the gods of historic Sheba. This occurred during the time of the Tanis dynasty that followed after the close of the Ramses dynasty that had enslaved the Hebrews.

The hunter Amun-Ra seeks the seven sisters or goddesses to rule over them. The number seven in scriptural texts has been referenced to the seven spirits of god, the seven character traits of God and the Seven Churches addressed in the book of Revelation. In each of these biblical representations, the image is strongly feminine in nature.

If this context is then considered, it would follow that Amun-Ra is seeking to rule over the seven churches identified in the beginning of the book of Revelation to again rise to power in these later days. The dove moon then comes to provide protection – perhaps symbolic of the Holy Spirit of YHWH or the ministry of the prophets also mentioned as coming in mass numbered to 144,000 in the book or Revelation.

Whatever the right interpretation may be, I pray these biblical prophets find their divine calling through the power of the Holy Spirit and make themselves ready for a 'battle of protection' of the true Church in the days to come. What we can conclude is these sisters are a female force who will need protection from the hunter of darkness.

Chapter 8: Meeting the Dove Sisters

Bluedove

With my experience of holding and reviving a Native American 'princess' in my dreams, I had gone for many many years not connecting this with anyone in the earthly world. I had spent the last 5 years in the mountains of Colorado West of Colorado Springs at 10,000 elevation in retreat writing books as a Franciscan monk.

The winters were very cold – below 30 below zero at times in the winter and this I found very difficult. I had a heart attack that resulted in open heart surgery and a triple bypass. After some recovery, I then decided to not winter there any more in addition I needed to pay off a $6000 note for the property to Catholic Charities. I had no income as a Franciscan Abbot then serving under the American Orthodox Patriarchate.

I decided to sell the sacred retreat property where I had received so many visitations and dreams about the future. I prayed to YHWH it would sell to people who could respect the sacredness of the area and carry on with the mission there.

I received a call from a Craig's List ad and met with a retired couple in Arkansas. They told me they wanted the property and it was their daughter who led them to the property. We worked out a down payment and monthly payment schedule and parted company. Before they left, I gave them a set of my 3 books then published on the rise of the New World Order.

I was told later the following story upon meeting their daughter a few weeks later who was traveling with them. She later told me that Bluedove was her Native name being of Cherokee and Blackfoot tribal origin. She then told me how she had a dream the night <u>before</u> I met her parents with a visitation of a bluish colored angelic entity with blond hair who approached her in a dream.

This blue angel was followed by a human looking woman with brown hair.

I was then told the blue angel moved closer and until she stood right next to Bluedove. With some frustration on her face the blue angel threw a book into Bluedove's lap and told her, "If you want to know what is going on, read the book!"

Bluedove then looked at the cover of the book in the dream and saw a circle and a bird-like symbol in the middle.

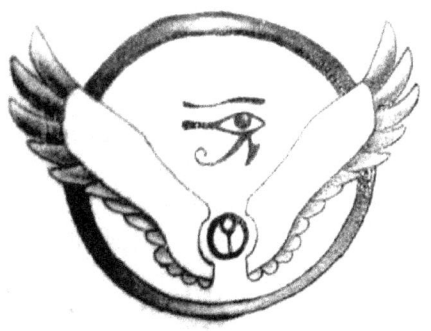

The next day, Bluedove shared with me that she met with her mother and found her reading a book. She noticed the cover of the book and saw that it was the same cover as the book she saw in her dream as given to her by the blue angel. She recounted how she was stunned and wondered what this meant for her. It was from this meeting that we became friends and this book has emerged as the Dove Prophecies.

Bluedove is a very beautiful woman of pale skin yet strong Native American features. She is 5'10" inches in height and looks 10 years younger than her age. I then naturally wondered who she might be. Was she the one I have been waiting for? I sent her the page numbers to read in the book about the dream called the 'Horse Woman' also included earlier in this book. I asked her to read the dream and tell me what she thought about it.

We talked the next day and she told me the horse woman was her. In this Horse Woman dream, many Native Elders were gathered for a ceremony where I received a horse and woman who became one.

Was she the Native princes of so many years ago I asked myself? Was it Bluedove and I who were now to be together hand in hand that would renew the forgotten covenant and bring back life to the native lands that were currently dry and barren?

I have since come to understand that Bluedove is one among many other Sisters of the Dove. The Native Princess was not just one woman but many woman divinely connected with mother earth who are called by YHWH as the Sisters of the Dove.

Bluedove had a later dream where she was with her pet turtle dove that she carried most everywhere on her shoulder. In this dream her dove was taken from her and it was later found to have been immersed in turpentine as if preserved by some well meaning children seeking to clean the bird. Sadly her beloved bird died in this dream.

The dream showed the dove being laid out in the sun and dried. Bluedove saw her dried dove who she loved had then become a symbol as a dove emblem. She was told in this dream that this symbol would last for 800 years.

The dove has become the symbol or emblem for the Sisters of the Dove.

It was about this time her real bird was caught by a cat in the dark hours of the morning and disappeared. This loss for Bluedove was devastating as this dove was her most favored friend. The intertwining of these two events both spiritual and physical were very tragic for her and now leaves a deep hole in her heart even to this day.

Meeting Moondove

Before meeting Bluedove, I met Moondove who is of Mohawk tribal origin in NY. She is a wonderful woman who is one of the most encouraging people I have ever met. Many times when I was given to disillusionment, my email chats with her pulled me out of the doldrums to take another run at life in embracing the bigger mission I have been given by YHWH.

She made up a name for me at the time as the Dovekeeper. In three dream cases over 35 years, I saw myself with a Native princess who was in an unconscious state as I held her head in my arms. I was to be there for her and pray that she might be healed and not die. The name Dovekeeper fits. This calling occurred long before the Sisters of the Dove were recognized by me or others as a divine Order. It was in meeting both Bluedove and Moondove that the Dove theme emerged in forming the Sisters of the Dove who were already a part of the Melkizedek Order having been given this call by YHWH himself.

Meeting Chardove

The third Sister of the Dove I have met is a woman in Colorado who I spent some time with in friendship. Chardove as I call her is one of the most loving people I have ever met. A magnitude of love and acceptance just flows from her eyes and being.

We often would go up into the mountain to a sacred grotto to give praise, offer incense to YHWH and pray. This was the same place where I had seen Michael the Archangel and where I was later instructed by him that we would have the support of the 4 armies of the angelic winds in the battle against the rise of the New World Order.

One night while asleep, I woke up to hear Chardove who was sleeping in the other room crying out for help. She could not move and her voice was barely heard. I began to pray and then she came to, shot out of bed and went outside in the night very angry denouncing her assailants.

She later told me she had been attacked by 4th dimensional Reptilian entities. Outside in the middle of the night, Chardove gave all entities that might have been lurking in the area the riot act and made sure they knew she was not to be a target in the future. It was great to see her so forceful against an enemy.

The next day she described the event in more detail. In her semi-awake dream state she had been attacked and bound by 2 very tall Reptilians who wore crowns. She knew they wanted to take her – abduct her for their own purposes. She was of the line of King David thus a Grail woman of this genetic line – a royal line. She knew these royal Reptilian brothers wanted to use her to create a hybrid race that could claim the right of kingship on the earth.

She related that as I began to pray, Y'Shua arrived with warrior angels. The battle resulted in this Royal class of Reptilians being cornered and captured. One of the Reptilians brothers resisted and was killed. The other was then seen by Chardove kneeling before the throne of Y'Shua and voluntarily laid his crown on the floor before Y'Shua in the throne room of YHWH. He was spared death because he had submitted to the authority of Y'Shua who is the King of Kings placed in this position by YHWH, who is the creator of all creators.

Chardove continues as a Sister of the Dove in advising and teaching other younger Sisters in the ways of YHWH and in the power of love. I have learned much from her and consider her advice very precious to me.

Other Sisters,

I now fully accept the existence of the Sisters of the Dove as a female Order as a complement within the Order of Melkizedek who are ordained by YHWH himself.

Abbot David Michael

    I continue to meet other Sisters of this anointing and calling who have had similar experiences and a sense of destiny as warriors and healers to bring peace and life back to the earth. They continue with the mission of Eve as mothers and healers of earth with some being complemented by a man and some as single women.

    The character of this Order is very tribal and embraces a merger of Hebrew-Native American culture in that this seems to have been it origin in times past – as early as 1000 BCE in the Americas during the reign of King David and King Solomon.

Chapter 9: Anishinabe [Anasazi] Ojibwe Prophecy of the 7 Fires

The Native American Mic-mac tribes are close cousins in historic alliance with the Ojibwe [Anishinabe] people and have unknowingly described the arrival of the Culdee (Hebrew Celtic Christians) in the pre-Columban era. They tell of the Culdee dressed in white robes walking and chanting in NE America long before the Vikings arrived in the 10th century.

The legend of St. Brendan the Navigator also known as a Culdee has him arriving with his companions in NE America in the 5th century. He as a Culdee (Hebrew-Celtic believer) is noted with founding Culdee communities in America between the 5th and 9th centuries. Sadly, these Hebrew-Christians were driven from their Eastern American villages by the Vikings after pillaging Iceland, Greenland, Labrador and Maine.

About the time of the arrival of the Culdee, the Ojibwe were in Maine and were given the 7 fires prophecies dating as early as the 5th or 6th centuries – possibly as early as 1000 BCE. These prophecies foretold the future of their people in the coming of the future holy and then the unholy white man.

The prophecy says their people would migrate West from the East due to the white people and identifies two separate groups of white people that would come – one good and the other evil. The prophecy is to follow.

The Seven Fires Prophecies of the Anishinabe [Anasazi]

First Fire

The first prophet said to the people, "In the time of the First Fire, the Anishinabe nation will rise up and follow the sacred shell of the Midewiwin Lodge.

The Midewiwin Lodge will serve as a rallying point for the people and its traditional ways will be the source of much strength.

The Sacred Megis will lead the way to the chosen ground of the Anishinabe [Anasazi?]. You are to look for a turtle shaped island that is linked to the purification of the earth. You will find such an island at the beginning and at the end of your journey.

There will be seven stopping places along the way. You will know the chosen ground has been reached when you come to a land where food grows on water. If you do not move you will be destroyed."

The second prophet told the people, "You will know the Second Fire because at this time the nation will be camped by a large body of water.

Second Fire

In this time the direction of the Sacred Shell will be lost. The Midewiwin will diminish in strength, a boy will be born to point the way back to the traditional ways. He will show the direction to the stepping stones to the future of the Anishinabe people.

Third Fire

The third prophet said to the people. "In the Third Fire, the Anishinabe will find the path to their chosen ground, a land in the west to which they must move their families. This will be the land where food grows on water.

Forth Fire

The Fourth Fire was originally given to the people by two prophets. They come as one. They told of the coming of the Light Skinned race.

One of the prophets said, "You will know the future of our people by the face the Light Skinned race wears. If they come wearing the face of brotherhood then there will come a time of wonderful change for generations to come.

They will bring new knowledge and articles that can be joined with the knowledge of this country, in this way, two nations will join to make a mighty nation. This new nation will be joined by two more so that four will form the mightiest nation of all.

You will know the face of the brotherhood if the light skinned race comes carrying no weapons. If they come bearing only their knowledge and a hand shake."

The other prophet said," Beware if the Light Skinned race comes wearing the face of death. You must be careful because the face of brotherhood and the face of death look very much alike. If they come carrying a weapon...beware. If they come in suffering... They could fool you. Their hearts may be filled with greed for the riches of this land. If they are indeed your brothers, let them prove it. Do not accept them in total trust.

You shall know that the face they wear is one of death if the rivers run with poison and the fish become unfit to eat. You shall know them by these many things.

Fifth Fire

The Fifth Prophet said, "In the time of the Fifth Fire there will come a time of great struggle that will grip the lives of all Native people.

At the warning of this Fire there will come among the people one who holds a promise of great joy and salvation. If the people accept this promise of a new way and abandon the old teachings, then the struggle of the Fifth Fire will be with the people for many generations.

The promise that comes will prove to be a false promise. All those who accept this promise will cause the near destruction of the people."

Sixth Fire

The prophet of the Sixth Fire said, "In the time of the Sixth Fire it will be evident that the promise of the Fifth Fire came in a false way.

Those deceived by this promise will take their children away from the teachings of the ELDERS, grandsons and grand-daughters will turn against the ELDERS.

In this way, the ELDERS will lose their reason for living... they will lose their purpose in life. At this time a new sickness will come among the people. The balance of many people will be disturbed. The cup of life will almost be spilled. The cup of life will almost become the cup of grief."

At the time of these predictions, many people scoffed at the prophets. They then had medicines to keep away sickness. They were then healthy and happy as a people. These were the people who chose to stay behind in the great migration of the Anishinabe. These people were the first to have contact with the Light Skinned race. They would suffer the most.

When the Fifth Fire came to pass, a great struggle did indeed grip the lives of all Native people. The Light Skinned race launched a military attack on the Indian people through-out the country aimed at taking away their land and their independence as a free and sovereign people. It is now felt that the false promise that came at the end of the Fifth Fire was the materials and riches embodied in the way of life of the light skinned race.

Those who abandoned the ancient ways and accepted this new promise were a big factor in causing the near destruction of the Native people of this land.

When the Sixth Fire came to be, the words of the prophet rang true as the children were taken away from the teachings of the ELDERS. The boarding school era of "civilizing" Indian Children had begun. The Indian language and religion were taken from the children. The people started dying at an early age... they had lost their will to live and their purpose in living.

In the confusing times of the Sixth Fire, it is said that a group of visionaries came among the Anishinabe. They gathered all the priests of the Midewiwin Lodge. They told the priests that the Midewiwin Way was in danger of being destroyed.

They gathered all the sacred bundles. They gathered all the scrolls that recorded the ceremonies. All these things were placed in a hollowed out log from the ironwood tree. Men were lowered over a cliff by long ropes. They dug a hole in the cliff and buried the log where no one could find it. Thus the teachings of the ELDERS were hidden out of sight but not out of memory.

It was said that when the time came that the Indian people could practice their religion without fear that a little boy would dream where the Ironwood log, full of the Sacred Bundles and Scrolls were buried. He would lead his people to the place.

The Seventh Fire

The Seventh Prophet that came to the people long ago was said to be different from the other prophets. He was young and had a strange light in his eyes. He said, " In the time of the Seventh Fire, New People will emerge.

They will retrace their steps to find what was left by the trail. Their steps will take them to the ELDERS who they will ask to guide them on their journey. But many of the ELDERS will have fallen asleep. They will awaken to this new time with nothing to offer. Some of the ELDERS will be silent out of fear.

Some of the ELDERS will be silent because no one will ask anything of them. The New People will have to be careful in how they approach the ELDERS. The task of the New People will not be easy.

If the New People will remain strong in their Quest, the Water Drum of the Midewiwin Lodge will again sound its voice. There will be a Rebirth of the Anishinabe [Anasazi?] Nation and a rekindling of old flames. The Sacred Fire will again be lit.

Commentary

In the forth fire and the fifth fire prophecy, two separate races would come and both were identified as being white. The first was a white race that came with no swords and the second had swords.

The first with no swords would join with the Ojibwe/Anishinabe as one people in peace and move west and teach them many things.

The second white race would come with swords and promise good things but deceive the Ojibwe/Anishinabe, steal their lands and children and seek to destroy their people.

As the Abbot General of the Order of the Culdee, I believe this prophecy is of YHWH and affirms that the Culdee were the first white people of Hebrew-Celtic origin of the 4th fire that brought peace with no sword and lived peaceably and in covenant among the Native Americans. This union eventually became by its decline known as the Anishinabe /Anasazi culture and nation.

According to archeological history, the migration of the Ojibwe/ Anishinabe is believed to have started in the area of Maine where they then traveled along the St. Lawrence River and settling around Lake Superior near the head waters of the Mississippi.

The name Mississippi originates from an Ojibwe word Miziziibi of the Algonquian language set. The head waters of the Mississippi River would have been known to the Ojibwe Anishinabe and it is very likely that the Ojibwe also traveled up and down the Mississippi for trade and hunting.

If accompanied by the Culdee who were by nature explorers, they would have explored many tributaries of the Mississippi including the Colorado and Arkansas Rivers.

Migration to the 4 Corners Area

Some of the Ojibwe would have remained in the Lake Superior area while others joining with the Culdee could have continued to migrate west to lands that were warmer and agriculturally productive.

The final homeland for this new Hebrew Celtic-Native American culture would be in the founding the city-kingdoms of the Anasazi that were known to exist between 800 AD and 1200 AD in the 4-corners area of the South West part of America in Utah, Colorado, Arizona and New Mexico.

Travel by water was much easier around 800 AD when the SW part of America had much more rain and rivers could be more easily navigated by boat. The lands where food grows on water could have been the Great Lakes region and later the floating gardens of the Anasazi.

Exploring up the Arkansas and Colorado Rivers would bring the nation into the 4-corners region of Utah, Colorado, Arizona and New Mexico where the most advanced Native civilization in North America was known to exist between 800 and 1200 AD.

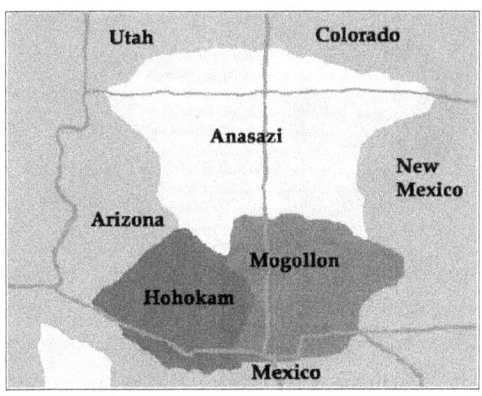

The map to the right shows the 4 corners region and outlines the known lands of the Anasazi.
Other maps show the Anasazi were farther north than what this map indicates including the Pikes Peak area of Colorado as the northern border. This same culture in its early years may have extended East down the Arkansas joining to the Mississippi.

Names of God

The name of the Ojibwe was created by the French with the original as Anishinabe. It was this name that appears to emerge for the new civilization that suddenly appeared in the 8th century called the the Anasazi by the Utes. There does seem to be a similarity between these two tribal names with the difference being due to language translation occurring between 2-3 languages.

It could very well be that the name Anasazi is a corruption of the original name of the Ojibwe that was Anishinabe as encountered by the French. The highest creator god of the Ojibwe was called Moni-to and the name of the Creator of the Anasazi was called Manitou which further suggests a cultural connection.

 The ancient symbol for the Anasazi Creator is a Celtic styled cross set in an 'X' style like a St Andrews cross (right). This same 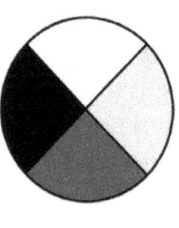 styled cross was found inscribed in stone at Los Lunas, N. Mexico and was worn by a carved figure with a crown. This cross due to its sacred association with Creator may be the origin of the 'Medicine Wheel' now used by many Native American tribes in prayers and healing.

The Ojibwe-Anasazi were likely joined by 2-3 other Native American nations as also prophesied in the 7 fires prophecies. This civilization was known through archeology to build aqueducts and cobble roads linking all of the major Anasazi cites separated by hundreds of miles.

They also built multi-storied castles in the style and methods also found in the Middle East and among the Celts. Among the ruins of the Anasazi, there is artifactual evidence of discarded dross from the smelting of iron. Saw marks on building timbers dating back 1000 years have been found and still exist in Anasazi castles at Hovenweep.

The decline of the Anasazi was circa the 12th century which is about the time when the Aztecs were known to have migrated north into the SW region of America. Some well meaning archaeologists have found evidence of cannibalism in Anasazi sites and suggest the Anasazi were cannibals. More likely this is evidence of the well-known rituals of the Aztecs left behind when conquering the declining Anasazi cities.

The Aztecs were known to eat 'parts' of their conquered enemies to seek to gain their powers. It may well be the Aztecs overran the remaining Anasazi cities while the bulk of the Anasazi people left earlier due to the decline in rainfall and climate warming that caused an extended drought and destroyed much of the agriculture and commerce in the 4 corners region.

Many tribes in the region such as the Pueblo, Hopi, Zuni and others claim descent from the Anasazi. The ratio of Culdee to Ojibwe-Anasazi would have been very small but intermarriage is likely to have occurred in bonding the two tribal peoples as one in covenant – at least among the families of the Native chiefs of the period and the Hebrew Celtic chiefs of the Culdee.

Covenant Still Exists

It is my belief that this early covenant between the Ojibwe/Anasazi and the Hebrew Culdee is still a valid covenant dating back over 1000 years as occurring as the 4th fire of the Ojibwe prophecy. I believe the 'land' of the 4-corners area of America still 'remembers' this covenant and wants to return to this covenant to again drink from its blessings as the 4th fire and then can become the 7th fire of the Ojibwe prophecy. It is a covenant originally sealed in blood through intermarriage and would take precedent over all other treaties ending in treachery that followed with the 'whites with swords' who came long after the Culdee.

I personally pray for the return of Native Americans to the Ojibwe-Anasazi and Hebrew Culdee covenant in these last days in fulfillment of the '7 fires' prophecies.

Chapter 10: Hopi Blue Kachina vs. Red Kachina

Kachina Prophets

The Hopi Kachina events prophesied for the future seem to be two separate events, representing two different powers with two different functions that will come to or appear on earth as foretold by the Hopi prophets.

The Hopi prophecy tells us the blue events and persons will come first then are closely followed by the red events and persons.

Blue Kachina

The Blue Kachina is described as a forerunner of the Red Kachina. This part of the prophecy identifies two companions or two prophets of Pahana [Messiah?] that will prepare the way for Pahana's return in seeking to bring the Native people back to the most ancient faith and God of their forefathers. Some suggest the Blue Kachina are the two prophets who are to precede the return of Pahana.

Red Kachina

The Red Kachina is described as a purifier that brings destruction or purging to the earth.

This purger of fire only effects those who have not received the teachings of the Blue Kachina prophets. This

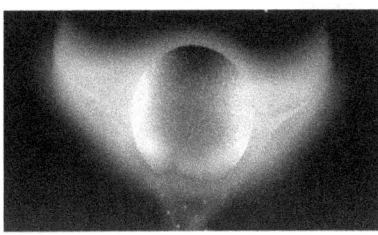

is a time of judgment for the unbelievers in YHWH.

Some versions of this prophecy understand the two coming Kachinas to be literal celestial events that will occur in the stars to herald their arrival. I believe this is also to occur.

After a trip to the Hopi Reservation and speaking with three medicine men of the Hopis, I have come to understand that the Blue Kachina is associated with water and the Red Kachina is associated with fire. The Blue Kachina will bring with it the promise of water to nurture the land. The Red will come with the fire of purging.

Red are RA Priests

The red symbol in the stars is in this researcher's opinion representative of Nibiru which when photographed is seen as red with wings.

Although the Red Kachina is positively viewed as a transformer or purifier by those that tend to follow the ancient Anunnaki gods, in ancient Hebrew records it is identified as a destroyer and sometimes named Wormwood.

In either case, it will create havoc upon the earth and force change among its inhabitants by global disasters of destruction.

I suggest the Nibiru Anunnaki are associated with RA and according to other dreams and prophecies we are receiving on this theme, he comes to seek to regain his rule as a task master over humanity and not as a servant-king.

RA in ancient reliefs in Egypt is represented as a circle with wings which is a stunning graphic representation of Nibiru. We are being shown that he will seek to rule over and destroy all who do not comply to his demands.

However, those who have heard the message of the two Blue Kachina prophets as the forerunner of Pahana will be provided a safe place by the Creator of creators known as YHWH or YaHuVeHa for their protection. These are often described by the Hopi as the lands that are still under their control such as the Reservation lands in the 4 corners area of America.

Some have considered the meaning of the arrival of Nibiru and RA as the beginning of the Biblical 4-horsemen of the Apocalypse which is covered elsewhere in my books.

Blue is the YHWH Priests

It is my understanding that the blue of the Pahana represents the priests of YHWH and with Messiah Y'Shua as the returning Pahana.

The Blue Kachina prophets that come before him are the companions of Pahana and share the message of Pahana prior to his return. The Bible in confirming this also speaks of two prophets who will come into the world in the last days to prepare the way for the return of Messiah.

It may be that these prophets are not literal individuals but two groups of people that come to renew the faith of the people in leading them back to the God of their forefathers in each continent.

I am of the opinion that the two people groups in America are the prophets and seers of the Native Americans as joined with the prophets and seers of the hereditary Hebrew priesthood. When rejoined as one people, we will witness the reemergence of the people of the Anasazi Covenant.

These will be joined in covenant to share a common teaching showing how the people of covenant began as one people from the beginning with a common faith, language and adoration toward Creator with a godly respect for nature. They will also bring with them the skills to bring water back to the land of the Native American such as the Hopi in showing they are of the Blue Kachina calling and anointing and not impostors.

Blue was always the color used by the Melchizedek priesthood and later the Hebrew priesthood in ancient times. Sometimes they were called the 'Blue Tunic Warriors' and even the high priests wore white robes with blue colored vestments over the top of the white.

Blue is the color associated with the Pahana, his prophets and not red. In the skies, blue may also be the 'eye' of the milky way that looks upon earth – some think the coming of heaven to earth.

Some have claimed that the star Sirius is the blue star but I have come to understand that Sirius has been compromised by the associated forces of RA and others in this alliance.

I am not convinced of any viable interpretation yet as to the event of blue that will appear in the heavens unless it is the sign of the Sisters of the Dove. However, I am assured that this blue does represent the angelic army of Creator that Michael the Archangel is leading. I have recently come to understand the Sisters of the Dove are female in gender and serve as blue warriors in this angelic conflict.

Deception Comes

I have also been shown that the red forces will make claim as the creators of mankind and say that RA is the Pahana or the Messiah and even the creator of mankind. He may even put on the blue cloak to cover over the red nature of his origin. I have read where this is now being taught on the internet by some shamans. I can tell you this is a deception.

Dove Prophecies

RA although being a creator of some humanoid species is not the Creator of Creators and did not create Adam and Eve as the god-man species that were given the priestly rule over the earth.

Many upon the earth have fallen and will fall into this deception and become slaves to his regime. I will also say as one who once wore the red robes of the Red Kachina as an Orthodox bishop (Roman Church of the East) , the red also represents the control of the Roman Church system and the enslavement of souls.

It is fear, anger, hate and the desire to kill that is the 4-fold path to deception that will give the Native American over to the judgment of the Red Kachina powers. Further, they will seek to kill those who have heard and received the word of the Blue Kachina prophets.

Masks Removed

According to Hopi prophecies, the masks of the Kachina dancers will be taken off and the world will see the dancers for who they really are.

I believe the Red Kachina will be seen for his true desire to rule the earth as a task master whereas the Blue Kachina will be seen as the Pahana companions in the joining of the Hebrew priesthood with the priesthood of the Native Americans.

The Blue Kachina prophets will teach the way of Creator and the language and music of Creator. Together with one voice, both native and white man will sing as one in drawing the enlightened people of both cultures under the one banner of protection by Creator (YHWH) leading them to 'safe places' that have been set aside for this purpose. I have concluded that Y'Shua is the Pahana that is returning to earth. The Hopi Tablets are the fall and redemption story of the Garden of Eden. More on this in following chapters.

This is a relatively new area of study for me so please if you have a different understanding, I would love to hear it. What I have presented above is my understanding thus far and is not set in stone. If I find information that leads in a different direction, I will immediately take the better direction that approaches the real truth that brings liberty to the spirit-soul.

Chapter 11: Origin of the Anasazi

It is my opinion that the Anasazi were such a culture of two races, the Hebrew Celts of 800 AD and the Native American. Even earlier research suggests that some of the Native tribes literally emerged from the Hebrews (10 tribes) coming to the New World as early as 1000 to 500 BC starting about the time of King Solomon as the nation of Israel fell into division.

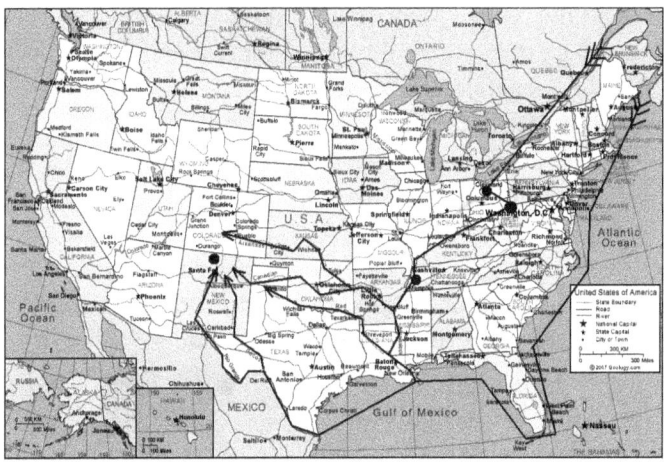

In the map above, this route is indicated by paleo-Hebrew inscriptions in stone (dotes on map) with some being the biblical 10 Commandments. Hebrew inscriptions have been found in Ohio, West Virginia, Tennessee and finally Los Lunas NM. showing the probable route of this migration.   This route that was taken by the Hebrews in 1000 to 500 BCE as the first migration into the Americas.

Abbot David Michael

If one considers the location of these Hebrew artifacts as indicating the migratory route of the early Hebrews, it portrays a map of the migration of the Hebrews ultimately to the 4-corners area some 1500 years later into Colorado, Utah, New Mexico and Arizona which became the land of the Anasazi and now the land of the Hopi, Navajo and Zuni as their descendants.

The first migration of the Celtic-Hebrews as a remnant of the 10 tribes began in 1000 BCE and continued until about 750 CE. The later migration merged with the earlier now Native American Hebrews and formed the Anasazi culture. It would appear the last migration of the Hebrew-Celts followed the same route as the first migration 1500 years later. (see map above)

Evidence for the fusion of Celtic-Hebrew and Native Culture Circa 800-1200 AD is compelling.

1. Castle building methods and materials is very similar to that used in Scotland and parts of Ireland during the era of the crusades.
2. Evidence of metal saw marks on structural roof timbers in Hovenweep castle structures date to 1200 AD.
3. Iron slag has been found in Anasazi dumps. Iron deposits have been found near many of the Anasazi cities.

4. pictograph of man with crown wearing Celtic cross brooch has been found near the Decalogue in Los Lunas, NM. The design of the brooch is clearly Celtic and was used by the Celts prior to the 9th century.

5. The Crown is of an Eastern origin worn by both 'bishops' (instead of a mitre) and 'chiefs' among the Celts prior to the 9th century. This Celtic brooch cross is believed to have become the design basis for the symbol to identify the deity Manitou, the "god without a face" and later the medicine wheel.

6. The design of the Kivas resemble common storage chambers used for grain and foods used by the early Hebrew-Celts of Ireland who originated from the Middle East. They first migrated to Ireland by the 5th century BC and later by the 4th century AD to the Americas.

7. Legends of the Mic Macs identify a religious group of white people chanting in procession wearing white robes. These Hebrew Christian Celts (Culdee) wore white robes and were noted as visiting the Americas as early as the 4th century with the voyage of Saint Brendan.

8. Evidence shows the Culdee (Hebrew-Christian Celts) were driven by the Norse from Scotland to Iceland by the 6th century and from Iceland to Greenland by the 7th century and then to the Americas by the 8th century. They were then driven from the East coast of the Americas west by the Vikings in the 9th century with the establishment of Vineland in the Americas. Old maps verify this migration.

9. The 7 prophecies of the Ojibwe identify a white race that joined with their people and brought peace prior to the arrival of Columbus in the 15th century. The Culdee carried no swords but were priests. The prophecies also speak of another white race that would come later and steal their lands and kill their children.

10. Ogham/Ogam (early Celtic script) writing is found near Cortez, Co that tells of a 'king' that lives near by with arrow pointing the way to his abode. Inscription dates to the Anasazi period.

11. Disappearance of the Anasazi occurred about the time of the migration north of the Aztecs who were ritually cannibalistic.

12. Evidence of cannibalism (human teeth marks on human bones) in ruins of Anasazi dwellings dates to this period circa the 13th century. Utes are said to be Aztec descendants whereas the Pueblo culture claim Anasazi descendancy.

13. There was discovered the Decalogue of the biblical 10 Commandments written in a proto-Hebrew script found in the 1830's in Los Lunas NM.
14. Such a Hebrew style of script was not known to academia until the 1890's. However, the inscription in Los Lunas NM discovered in the 1830's based on rock patinas suggests an origin circa the 12th century.
15. The Ojibwe history speaks of a migration from the East coast to the land of the turtle (Great Lakes) before the arrival of Columbus. It is believed that they then with the Celts migrated south down the Mississippi and then up the Arkansas or Colorado river to the 4-corners area.
16. It is also suggested that migrations occurred also up the Colorado and the Mississippi to the Arkansas via the Gulf of Mexico. There is evidence that both the Colorado and the Arkansas Rivers were navigable into the 4 corners area by boat well into the 12th century. It is now no longer the case due to a drying climate.
17. Welsh speaking 'Indian' tribes were discovered by many early explorers in the SE coasts of America and as far West as the North West Territory by the Louis and Clark expedition. What is Welsh today, is likely the common Celtic form prior to the 6th century when the Celtic migrations to America began.

18. Ancient Welsh has an unprecedented number of Hebrew words in the language suggesting an origin or strong cultural connection to the Hebrew people. Modern Hebrew has little resemblance to ancient spoken Hebrew so it is difficult to determine what is Welsh and what is Hebrew since the script is different.

19. Inscriptions of a rider and horse predate the arrival of Columbus in the four coursers area. The Culdee would have brought horses with them.

There is more compelling evidence that needs to be addressed. My work with the Vatican for 25 years made me privy to the history of the Culdee of which I am the Abbot General of this Hebrew Celtic Order. I am also a Hebrew by birth of the line of King David.

Chapter 12: Translating the Hopi Tablets

Language Script

In one of the Hopi Prophecies provided by Chief Whitefeather in 1958, it is foretold that the forgotten language of Pahana (Messiah) that is written in stone will once again be taught to the Native American. The script of the language is written on the sacred stones of the Pahana that are still held by the Hopi.

It is interesting to note that this same language script is seen inscribed on stones in Ohio, Colorado, New England and elsewhere across America. The estimated era of the formation of this language predates the Tower of Babel where the Bible tells us there was just one language and then during the building of the tower, the languages were divided.

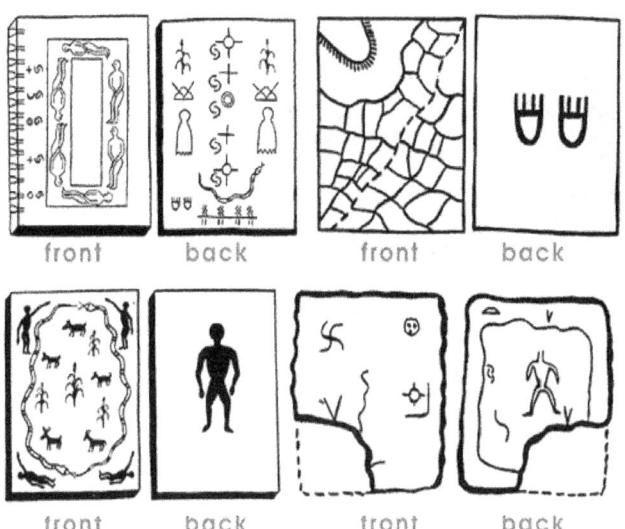

The 4 Hopi Tablets above are the key to understanding the future for the Hopi people and all Native Americans. Let's see what they might be telling us.

I will admit this is an attempt to translate and as such, is subject to debate. I do not claim to be corect in this translation but it is the best that seems to be right in considering the origin of the script of the Hopi Tablets.

Negev Hebrew in Colorado

One of the evident languages found in the Four-Corners area including Colorado, Utah, Arizona and New Mexico was an ancient paleo-Hebrew script as indicated by the chart on the next page. This Negev Hebrew dates as early as 1000 BCE perhaps arriving in the first migration or as late as 800-1200 CE as found among the Anasazi region in the last migration.

This may not have been used by all Natives in the area but certainly was used by a priestly class that were cited for inscribing the Decalogue (Ten Commandments) in Los Lunas, New Mexico dating to at least 1200 CE or earlier.

Research needs to be continued in deciphering these texts found scattered upon the cave walls of areas located near the Anasazi cities and villages.

Older Priesthood

I believe this priestly class represented the biblical Order of Melchizedek and not the Aaronic priesthood. They did have the 10 commandments given to them by Moses as indicated by the presence of the Decalogue carved in stone in Los Lunas, New Mexico.

Many scripts are found in the Americas. The most ancient seem to be the Proto-Hebrew or Sumerian script.

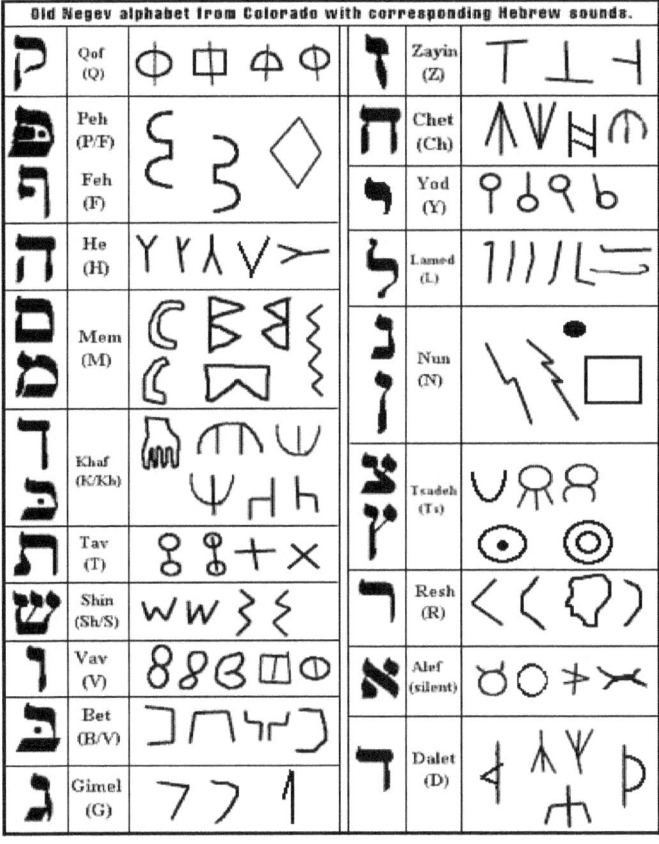

This is not the Mormon version of this priesthood but one that dates much earlier than the supposed and debated revelations of Joseph Smith. Other cult groups use the name Melkizedek name for their priesthood but this may not be a correct usage.

Y'Shua (Jesus) was of this Melchizedek priesthood as indicated by Paul in the Bible and this priesthood was primarily a priest-prophet calling given to the first born male of every Hebrew family.

Most Ancient Script

Some call this script in the chart above as Saharan or proto-Hebrew and others ascribe names to this script that reflects the country or region where it was found. Some suggest this original language script was first used among the earliest Sumerians before cuneiform evolved as given to them by the gods called the Anunnaki.

I suggest it was given to them by the angelic messengers of YHWH.

First Tablet, Front

The first tablet is simple and is related to the 4th tablet. Side one has six figures lying around a rectangular table inside of a fence. There are 5 symbols to the left of the table with 'some time later' marks to the left of each symbol.

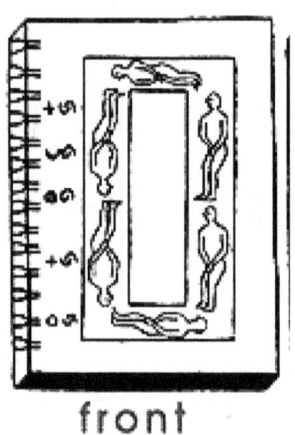

front

Dove Prophecies

The symbols need to be read from the bottom up. They begin with a circle, then a cross followed by a cross in a circle and then a curve and ending with another cross. It is a transition of time – perhaps a later translation of similar meaning with the symbols in the center of the tablet on the back. I believe these symbols represent vast periods of time associated with the stars.

First Tablet, Back

On the back of the tablet one is a primary series of symbols that begin at the bottom as a row of four glyphs on a line then a serpent followed by a circle with outside cross.

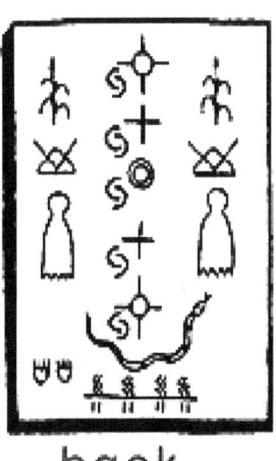

back

Then a cross then a circle in a circle in the center of the tablet. The 6th symbol up from the bottom is another simple cross and then ending at the top center with a circle with an outside cross.

These center symbols again appear to be the recording of a cycle of time associated with the stars or heavens. The bear paws appear to be the signature of the author or the name of the clan that protects these tablets.

First Tablet Translation

The front side of the first tablet with 6 men suggests 6 different creations of man possibly dating back 350,000 years. However, only four seem to have survived into modern times.

Abbot David Michael

On the back side of the tablet, my initial interpretation is the first symbol is the earth with the four glyphs as being four of the seven creations of humanoid man. The serpent is the claimed creator of one or more of these species of man and makes claim upon him. This may be the Massau serpent god of the Hopis.

The claimed serpent creator on this tablet offers spiritual or eternal life (ghost glyphs), well being and children (V and mound glyphs) and food (corn glyph) in exchange for their total obedience to him. This serpent is not the Creator of Creators but a lessor creator who claims to be God and uses deception to gain control over human souls.

Second Tablet

The second tablet is a map of a location of sacred significance. There are no symbols on this tablet except for what appears to be bear paws on the back.

However, you also find these bear claws on the first tablet above suggesting a people connection between these two tablets.

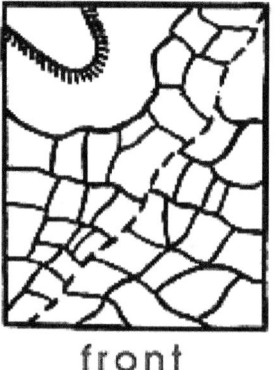

front

I would suggest tablet one predates the second tablet by hundreds perhaps thousands of years. I am inclined to think the author of this map is connected with the Anasazi people in identifying a place of importance. Perhaps a sacred mountain with the division of the land made for crops with a stream or river (doted line) running from north to south.

Dove Prophecies

back

More likely, the map was drawn facing East toward the rising sun and the mountain is a sacred 'mesa' type mountain. I would suggest that if this mountain can be found, a great store of artifacts that reveal the origin of the Native peoples and their original God(s) and culture would be found.

front

Third Tablet, Front

The third stone tablet is the creation story of the creation of man before Adam and Eve were created in the Garden of Eden. The double snake is the perimeter fence of the pre-Eden world.

Early man may have been placed under the care of the serpent Sama-el to provide for them but the serpent later rebelled against the Creator of all Creators named YHWH and then sought to make man his own people Among the Hopis, this serpent appears to be called Massau.

The 4 persons around the garden are considered to be the four human races or the four worlds that were created by various demigods. These humans predate the creation of Adam by YHWH who was then placed in the garden.

The double snake is a double helix or a double Ormus and has multiple meanings. It does represent the dual nature of man. It as an Ormus also suggests the perpetual life of the the species of many one being born – dying and then reborn as the next generation.

Third Tablet, Back

The back of the third tablet shows the creation of Adam as the god-man to be placed in the Garden of Eden for his protection. This was a new creation and he was created as a god of the earth and the cosmos. A royal priesthood who would rule over all other humanoid and animal creations.

back

Forth Tablet, Front

The forth tablet is the most important tablet and reveals the events that caused the separation of man from Creator. It is simply tells of the event of Adam and Eve leaving (YHWH) and the Garden of Eden and his promised future return.

It is this Tablet that has the corner removed. It is said he who returns this corner is thought to be sent by the true Pahana to lead the Native people back to the God of their forefathers and is not an impostor.

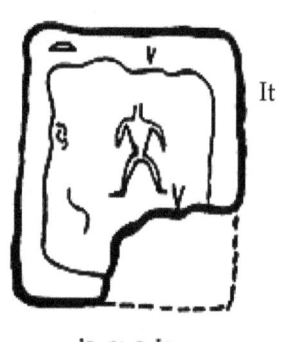

It

back

It is on this tablet like the first tablet that proto-Sumerian script is found suggesting both were made circa the same era of time by the same priesthood using the same language script. I would suggest these tablets could date to 1000 BCE.

This form of script provided as glyphs provides a complete idea with each symbol and not the use of phonetic sounds common to most modern languages. Many of the most ancient languages are read from the bottom up like the growth of a tree. For translation, I will read the sequence from the bottom to the top.

The first symbol event is missing – perhaps? We do not know if there is a symbol on this mission corner. Each of the glyphs represent a sequence of periods that must occur before the return of Pahana. Some have occurred and others are yet to occur.

Serpent and Woman Blamed

Reading up from the bottom, what we first see is a snake (curved line) and a 'V' symbol.

The fall of man and the leaving of Creator YHWH came as a result of the serpent who enticed the woman and deceived her and thus mankind fell from fellowship with the Creator of Creators named YHWH.

The garden shows a fence around the man but the 4 angels of protection are gone and the serpent life of the fence is gone since the serpent was cursed by YHWH for deceiving Eve and Adam. The head of the man Adam is gone suggesting he has lost his spirit-soul (has endured spiritual death) due to his rebellion against YHWH.

The serpent is blamed for this fall of man along with the woman who is represented by the 'V'. As we move toward the top of the tablet, we see the squiggly symbol of 'change over time' and then outside the fence is a bow and another 'V'.

The bow at the top represents an opposing human life force with a female species who will seek to destroy this fallen creation of Adamic man. I believe this force of the bow as the Hunter Orion is the Nephilim race birthed in Cain with Eve who are seeking to destroy the Adamic species of man to claim the priesthood of earth. In this the genocide of Adamic man began just after Adam and Eve were put out of the Garden and began with the murdering of Abel by Cain.

Forth Tablet, Back

On the listed front side (really the back side) we find the head that was missing from the other side of the tablet at the top right. The head represents the living 'spirit-soul' of man that was lost due to a separation from the life-sustaining ways of Pahana/YHWH.

It is implied the head will be found in the future in that it remains on the reverse side of the tablet and is not gone completely. This head or Adam's living spirit soul will be returned to the Adamic man by the messiah (Pahana) when he returns.

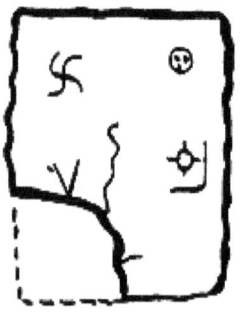

front

The head rests among other important symbols foretelling what events must come before the return of Messiah/Pahana. These symbols are events that must occur and also virtues that must be found before the head (spirit-soul) is joined back with the body of Adamic man.

Sequence of Events

The symbols begin to the bottom left with the first symbol being missing (perhaps?) but then comes the V. Then we see the serpent followed by the circle with cross lines in an L shape glyph. Then follows the right pointing swastika at the top left and finally the head to the top right.

The V is the woman and the need for reconciliation as the human female as an equal partner with man. Only then can the serpent be overcome (jumping over or stepping upon it) in bringing peace to heaven (circle with cross line) and earth (90 degree line) below.

When there is peace (unity) between heaven and earth, the life represented by the swastika will begin to again 'turn' or rotate with life and in this will be the enlightenment of understanding for the Adamic man, the Native American and all humans who are being saved from the deception and bondage of the serpent.

The right pointed swastika is found all over the world in many civilizations and it represents blessing and life whereas the Nazi Swastika (left point) is backwards life and thus draws its power from the dark side – perhaps the Nephilim enemy of man.

When life is found again, the head of man as his his spirit-soul will be found and be reconnected with the body of man.

Abbot David Michael

      The missing symbol(s) on this tablet are intriguing. Perhaps it reveals when all this will occur? Perhaps there is no other symbol at all – just a blank space. In any case, the evidence that the true Pahana has come is not agreed upon by the Native Americans. Perhaps the real evidence is in the Blue Kachina bringing life (water) back to the land before the return of the Pahana. Is the return of water to the land the sign of the Blue Kachina and the coming of the Pahana?

Chapter 13: Prophecy-Alliance between Ephraim, Judah and Native Americans

As I was awakening on the morning of the 10th of February, 2008, I heard the call of God go forth over America calling for an alliance to be forged between the princes of Ephraim and Judah and the Chiefs of the Native Americans. It was also shown that this alliance shall be in preparation for more difficult times that are to come to America and to the world.

The unity of the 12 tribes of Israel has not existed since the time of King Solomon. Generally today Judah still hates Ephraim and Ephraim views Judah with contempt. 'Jews' running the State of Israel have sought to give the God-apportioned land (Kingdom) of Ephraim (Shiloh) to the Palestinians thus widening the gap for unity between Judah and Ephraim. This may not be the full reality since many that call themselves Judah (Jews) are not Jews by blood but by conversion and are not of the seed of Jacob (Israel).

Extensive historical research as confirmed by yDNA testing has determined that a large majority of the modern Ashkenazi Jews originated from a mass conversion of the Khazars in circa the 10th century. These Khazars are descended from Edomites (of the line of Esau) and the Turks. It may be true that their daughters have intermarried with male Israelite Jews of the seed of Jacob yet they have no yDNA connection to Jacob (Israel) whatsoever.

Some have noted that such a dominance of blood Jews by Khazars (they run modern Israel today) are the descendants of Esau seeking to infiltrate the genetic bloodline of true Israel and reclaim the birthright that he lost to Jacob (Israel) in exchange for a bowl of lentils. With this Khazar infusion came also the heresy of Kabbalism.

However, I have observed that many of the blood Jews of the seed of Abraham, Isaac AND Jacob are at peace with Ephraim and many yDNA Jacob Jews have come to accept Y'Shua as Messiah who has united the remnant of true Judah and Ephraim.

As to the call for alliance with Native Americans, it is to be an alliance of blood via marriage and/or ritual. Many Native American tribes believe they have a blood connection to the Biblical Hebrews and some seek to reclaim the birthright of this origin. Bringing history a little closer to our modern times, the princes of Ephraim have predominately been living among the tribal Celtic peoples for the last few thousand years.

There is now compelling archeological evidence (still ignored by grant-paid archeologists) that the 4-corners Anasazi people were in fact a cohabitation (alliance) between the Hebrew-Celt (Ephraim/Judah) and the Native American circa 800-1200 CE. It is my belief that it will be with the Native American tribes who believe they are descended from the Anasazi that such an alliance will be most readily forged.

Chapter 14: The Curse of the Buffalo Beast

The Dream

In a dream of the 10th of January 2013, I found myself in an open field at dusk upon a high prairie which is where I lived when receiving this dream. Running toward me was a massive bull buffalo that looked more monster than buffalo. Its face was greatly exaggerated and great anger was in its red piercing eyes. I fought the beast by evading his attempts to crush and run me over. In time the buffalo beast gave up and left.

Very much relieved I suddenly heard the words in the dream, "Do not reap where you have not sown lest you bring a curse upon yourself." I then awakened.

Interpretation

In reflecting upon the dream, I understood the buffalo beast was symbolic of the earth's natural forces that would rise up against anyone who would take from the earth without caring for the earth. This principle also applies to business in dealing with others.

If we take from a business deal more than what is considered fare or reasonable for what we sowed into it, we are bringing a curse upon ourselves. By so doing we will unleash the buffalo beast against us. We cannot take advantage of another in business even if it is legal. If we do, the earth forces will rise up against us to curse us and bring us to nothing.

This seems to be a law forged into the fabric of creation from which there is no escape. This is a truth I am learning and have been warned about in my dealings with others. I am now going back to many I have taken advantage of and seeking to remedy what they perceive to be a business injustice.

Chapter 15: Dream – Ark of the Covenant in America

The Dream

In a dream of the night on March 14, 2014, I found myself at the foot of a great mountain. The land was forested but lacking large amounts of water. I thought later the location of the dream events were near Mt Nebo or Mt Magazine in Arkansas but the dryness of the area suggested elsewhere. This may have been a dream for sometime in the future when the land was more dry than it is now in the Mt Nebo and Mt Magazine area. It may have been a location in the 4-corners area rather than Arkansas. I have yet to have a clear sense of exact location.

As I looked up from the South standing at the base of this mountain, I saw a gully up the mountain with small scattered pools of water. It seemed that this gully was once a strong flowing stream but now only captured water in pools when it rained. The sides of the gully were rather steep but not cliffs with trees growing up the banks as far as the eyes could see. The pine looking trees were naturally spaced about 8 – 20 feet apart which suggests a dryer type of climate than Arkansas. The mountain was a mesa type mountain and flat on top.

Trail of 1000 Years

As I was looking up the gully, I heard the voice of an angel who said, **"The trail of 1000 years."** I never saw the angel but I intuitively knew I had to walk this trail back 1000 years to discover what needed to be known about the Holy people of YHWH once living in this area.

While still in the present, I then saw a man in American uniform standing among the trees who I understood to be a General connected to the dark forces of the US Shadow Government. He was looking at me and appeared to be agitated and resistant to my being there and certainly did not want me to pursue any search up the gully.

I knew the General wanted to get the artifacts himself but I sensed he could not find them since he was not appointed by YHWH to do so. I understood the artifacts to be related to the Ark of the Covenant brought to the new world for safety. It was now hidden and protected by angels. This was to the Generals much frustration.

1000 Years in the Past

I then found myself 1000 years earlier with the general gone from the dream. I was in the same place looking up the gully and saw the original large stream and a waterfall. This would place me back into the year 1014 during the rule of the Romanized 5th Kingdom of Calalus in America of Hebrew origin.

As I looked up the gully at the waterfall, I started walking up the gully and saw a waterfall about 20' tall cascading down over the rocks. I was drawn by the Spirit to the area behind this waterfall where a cave was located and the resting place of very important Hebrew artifacts – perhaps even the lost Ark of the Covenant.

I was then able to see through the water and the covering rocks into a cave behind the water fall that protected the artifacts with the waterfall helping discourage discovery and access. I saw what I thought to be the Ark of the Covenant that was the original one made by Moses.

Knights Protecting Ark

Still in the past, I then noticed other men around me. They were dressed in early medieval armor and appeared to be guarding the site from intruders. They were assigned to guard the artifacts until the day these holy relics would be needed by true Israel sometime in the distant future.

Why were these artifacts carried to and hid in America I wondered to myself? How did they get here from Israel? Some legends speak of the prophet Jeremiah taking the Ark and other artifacts from Jerusalem just before it was overrun by Babylon and taking them to Ireland in circa 500 BCE.

Other legends say from Ireland, they were taken by Jeremiah to a 'new Israel' in America and this new Hebrew Kingdom was later called Avalon during the time of King Arthur (6th century) and Calalus during the time of Charlemagne (8th century).

This dating in the dream would place the knights in the 6th Kingdom of Calalus circa 800-1100 AD with the kings related to the 1st kingdom circa 1000 BC existing during the time of Solomon.

Israelite Kingdoms in America

I began to understand there had been many Hebrew kingdoms in America in this area of the Arkansas River basin spanning the last 3000 years. Each of these kingdoms were Hebrew in origin and ruled by the descendents of King David of Israel.

The first being the Kingdom of Solomon in circa 1000 BCE. The 2nd Kingdom occurred during the time of Jeremiah in 500 BCE with the 3rd about 140 CE. The 4th Kingdom occurred about 500 CE during the time of King Arthur of the Hebrew Celts with the 5th Kingdom occurring in 750-1100 CE as Calalus.

The rise of the 6th Kingdom is soon to occur as the Kingdom of the Melkizedek with the final 7th kingdom occurring at the return of King Y'Shua during the 1000 year millennial reign of Christ.

Calalus Knights

Now I found myself standing among these knights who were in America 1000 years ago. I seemed to be counted among them as their 'brother in arms' as we smiled and nodded to each other.

The helmets and armor they wore were a mix of Spartan, Roman and Celtic armor. Mail was not worn but small scale armor was more commonly seen with larger plates over the chest and shoulders.

Destruction of Calalus

Upon awakening, I wondered at the importance of the 1000 years ago date. I did a search on the year 1014 in Google and discovered that during that year on September 28th, two massive fragments of an asteroid hit the Atlantic and the Gulf of Mexico seas. The impact caused massive tsunamis and the destruction of the coastal areas of the Atlantic and Gulf and up the Mississippi and the Arkansas rivers. A chain reaction from the impacts caused volcanic eruptions which destroyed Mayan cities in Central America. http://peopleoffire.com

One can only wonder if this was a judgment of YHWH or perhaps a war of the gods with the Kingdom of Calalus targeted for its allegiance to YHWH. Perhaps it became vulnerable due to its fallen state in embracing Roman doctrines and authorities. This event and date recorded in science coincides with the sudden disappearance of the Anasazi people of the 4 corners area of SW America which is at the source of the Arkansas River and it feeder rivers in about 1000 CE.

Rise of the 6th and 7th Kingdom

It would appear the 6th kingdom of Avalon-Calalus is now being established (first in the heavenlies) with the alliance of many Native Americans as served by the Melkizedek priesthood of the line of King David.

Many tribes of Native Americans have Hebrew genetic origins and some among them are also called as Melkizedek priests for these end times.

I can only pray for a good foundation upon the true teaching of Y'Shua and the Holy Apostles in embracing the true faith of the Sabbath (Saturday) and the Holy Days of the annual cycle. This is a Kingdom led by those of the bloodline of King David and who have been called by YHWH into the Melkizedek priesthood. It is to this Hebrew Kingdom that the Ark of the Covenant will be given for their protection. Let's consider the 7 Hebrew Kingdoms in America in more detail.

First Kingdom: (Circa 1000 BC)
This is during the era of King David and Solomon. It is believed that gold and copper were mined in the Americas by Solomon and referred to in some texts as Solomon's Mines. Many Hebrew artifacts have been found dating to the era especially in the Ohio area and along the St. Lawrence River basin with copper mines dating to this period.

Second Kingdom: (circa 500 BC)
The second kingdom was thought to be established by Jeremiah or his servants in escaping the rule of Babylon in Israel. Jeremiah brought with him Temple artifacts (perhaps the Ark) and the Stone of Destiny to Ireland. Some researches believe the ark was then carried to the New World as the New Jerusalem by Jeremiah during his life time while other suggest later during the time of King Arthur.

Third Kingdom: (circa 140 AD)
This 3rd revival that became known as the Kingdom of David was reestablished by the family of Y'Shua and Joseph of Arimathea.

This Joseph of Arimathea was considered by some historians the half brother of Y'Shua called James the Just and was not an uncle. This was under the domain of a Hebrew-Christian kingdom that ruled in Britannia called the Culdee by the seed of King David that spilled over into the New World.

The location of Solomon's mines were known to the house of David and they would have opted to continue with mining in the new world in the new millennium. Joseph was known to be a miner of tin in Britain and to also mine other metals in the new world such as copper an gold is reasonable.

Forth Kingdom (circa 500 CE):

Again the Hebrew kingdom was reestablished then called Avalon by the the Knights of King Arthur. King Arthur was wounded in battle in circa 540 CE about the time other asteroid fragments were reported to have impacted earth causing a short term ice age destroying crops and cities around the world.

This Kingdom ruled over the lands of the Olmecs/ Toltecs according to historic records as protected by the Swan Knights of King Arthur. At this time, this Kingdom may have been called Avalon to which Arthur was taken by the daughters of the Queen of Septimania when wounded with the promise he would return one day to rule again over the Hebrews in the British Isles in freeing them from their English masters.

Fifth Kingdom: (circa 750-1100 AD)

Reestablished by the line of King David now associated culturally with Rome during the period of Charlemagne of the Holy Roman Empire.

It is not clear how much of the Roman influence was carried to the new world by the Romanized Hebrews of this era. From the records found in Arizona, this kingdom was not strong and had many Native enemies.

This kingdom ruled over the lands of the Toltecs and seemed to be a departure of the Hebrew way in embracing Hellenist tradition and polity. In its decline in 1014, this Hebrew people had married among the Native people with this remnant people of the 5th kingdom becoming known as the Anasazi.

Sixth Kingdom: (2014)

The sixth kingdom is now to be reestablished by the lineage of King David in preparation for the coming of Messiah-King Y'Shua. It is the Melkizedek priest-knights who will cause this Hebrew Kingdom to occur in the renewal of an ancient covenant between the Hebrew line of King David and the Hebrew Native American priesthood.

This covenant is a renewal of the 5th Kingdom covenant also referred to in the Ojibwe prophecy of the seven fires identified as the 4th fire.

Seventh Kingdom (near future)

The final Melkizedek ruled kingdom in America will occur with the return of Y'Shua who will rule over all of the earth from Jerusalem and over Avalon-Calalus-America as his chosen lands outside of Israel for 1000 years during the Millennium.

It is during this 1000 year reign of the world by Y'Shua that Avalon-Calalus-America will become a prominent power once again.

Under the guidance of the Melkizedek leadership, America will again become a land of plenty with every man having his own land and eating of the fruit of his labors in peace and living to a very old age. No war, disease or darkness will exist during this time as the earth is redeemed for the wars of destruction known as the Great Tribulation.

At the end of the 1000 years, another test will occur when Satan, aka the great dragon, will be released for a short period to test those who had been born during this time. A world war will again erupt but when it is finished, Satan and all darkness will be cast into eternal darkness forever. Then a new heavens and earth will be created for the people of faith, love and peace to live together into eternity.

Chapter 16: Visitation- Army of the 4 Winds

On Christmas day, December 25, 2010, I was up upon the mountain at 10,000 feet elevation most of the day praying and had a conversation with a representative of God (YHWH). I thought first it was the Holy Spirit as the conversation was in the mind yet very loud, vivid and distinct.

It was not casual thought or mental wanderings but later I was shown it was the Spirit of the Lord speaking through Saint Michael the Archangel who spoke to my understanding telepathically. The message was regarding the 4 winds that are among the armies of YHWH who will war against the regime of the antichrist in the last days.

Cross that Conquers

Some of the conversation I cannot fully disclose but I will share what I can. The event occurred as a series of conversational questions and answers and I was fully aware of my surroundings during the conversation. I knew where Michael the Archangel was sitting on a rock near to my left above me as he told me these things but I could not see him with my eyes.

The first question I posed was regarding the medicine wheel cross or St. Andrews cross that I had been told to use many years ago. I was told in a dream, "With this cross you will conquer." I saw a vision of the Saint Andrews cross as I was being told this. Here is the conversation with Michael the Archangel.

Q: Why was it said, "With this cross you will conquer?"
A: It is the symbol for the four winds. I will give you the 'protection' of the 4 winds. They are an army.
Q: Is that why I was called 'Windwalker' by the angels in a dream where I looked down upon the earth and saw the coming foreign troops invading America?
A: Yes. This name and call was known to them some time ago. Music will be the language to speak to the four winds. You have had this prophetic 'music' language gift since your fast upon Mount Zion when you were age thirteen. It is for this reason that the 'wind' angels have sang with you in worship on many occasions.
Q: How many are there in the army?
A: Twelve legions of angels are assigned to the four winds.
Q: How are they structured as an army?
A: There are 4 Generals leading each of the 12 winds and they are represented to man in dreams and visions in the form of horses that often speak. You met one of them in 1982. The four winds are represented as companies of red, black, white and dappled horses. Each wind has three Captains under the four Generals with one legion of angels assigned under each Captain. The 12 Captains under the 4 Generals have taken the names for each of the 12 tribes of Israel.
Q: What about the staff that I have proposed? What kind of material should be used for the coil tip or focal point?

A: That which transcends time and matter.

Thoughts

The conversation then ended and Michael the Archangel was gone from the rock where he was sitting. I subsequently did an extensive study of the scriptures to determine if what was spoken aligned itself with what has been revealed in the past. I came across 25 scriptures that related to this conversation. The major scriptures that confirmed what was spoken are as follows:

Scriptures Of the wind as an Army of YHWEH

1. Four winds are represented as horses of four different colors. Zec. 1
2. Wind horses travel the earth assessing the state of peace or war upon the earth. Zec. 6:5
3. Angels have a charge to protect us. Ps. 91:11
4. The Son of man [Y'Shua] sent forth his angels – angels under his command. Mat 13: 41
5. Twelve legions available to aid the cause of Y'Shua and the Saints. Mat 26:53
6. Angels gather the elect from the four winds. Mat 24:31
7. We (sanctified man) will judge angels. 1Cor 6:3
8. Four angels [generals] are given the command over the winds. Ez 6
9. Angels are ministering spirits sent forth to minister (serve) the heirs of salvation... Heb 1:4

10. Be hospitable... you may entertain angels unaware. Heb 13:2
11. Four Angels [generals] over four winds holding them back. Rev. 7:1
12. Twelve angels have power to hurt the earth in battle. Rev. 7:3
13. Told to prophecy to the four winds to breath life into the slain. Ez 37:9
14. Winds come from the treasure trove of God. Ps 135:7, Ps 18:10
15. Four winds cause earthly kings/kingdoms to rise or fall. Dan 7:2
16. God causes his winds to blow. Ps 147:18, Ps 135:7
17. God gathers the wind(s) in his fist. Prov. 30:4
18. Winds can divide the seas. Is 11:15
19. God will rebuke the nations with the winds. Is 17:13
20. Winds thresh the mountains [earth]. Is 41:15, Is 57:13
21. Wind can ravage the walls [fortresses] with water, fire and hailstones. Ez 13:13
22. The wind carries away the broken iron and clay [Antichrist alliance] crushed by Y'Shua. Dan 2:35

Thoughts

Based in the scriptures, all that I heard has been confirmed in this conversation except the 12 tribal names given or adopted by the 12 Captains and the use of music as the tool to bring the armies of the four winds to engage in battle. However this being true makes sense to me.

Evidence for music as the language of the winds is seen in the battle of Jericho that was engaged through the music of praise and worship. It is clear that music will be a part of bringing down the strongholds of the enemy. Further, if the winds or angels are to be judged by the heirs of salvation, we are given a relationship of command over angels as we walk in obedience to YHWH and Y'Shua as an heir to salvation.

As a warning, if we step from the center of this call, we have no power whatsoever over angels and we will likely fall into the hands of the enemy.

Number of Angels

A Roman legion in history was from 3000-6000 men. If the angel were numbered as 12 legions, this would be as many as 6000 X 12 which is 72,000 warrior angels. At Glentivar, a sister saw a small company of these warrior angels of the winds who were about 12' feet tall, fully armored with shields and swords and were about 120 in number. These she said were assigned to us to guard us.

Transcends Time and Matter

The last question and answer regarding the question of the making of the staff: "That which transcends time and matter," is yet to be fully revealed. What I do know I am not to disclose at this time. There is some evidence for all this with the work of 19th century scientist by the name of Keely that rivaled Tesla in discoveries and intelligence.

I can say the staff of YHWH will be a tool in the hands of the singer-prophets in the days ahead. Some have thought it is the staff of Moses that is being suggested here.

For My Salvation

I must admit that I was living in retreat in Colorado as led by dreams and visions to seek my own salvation in trying to humble myself before the Creator of Creators who is YHWH. I also realize that there are others who are like me who also have this deep sense of mission and destiny and are being trained elsewhere in the world. These are the people I am now seeking to find and pray for weekly upon the mountain as I offer incense to YHWH upon a simple rough stone altar I have built there.

It should be understood that our salvation (safety) from what will soon come upon the earth will be given to anyone who 'wills' to understand what Creator is seeking for us to understand.

To understand, we all must put aside our anger and mistrust of the past and draw together in one covenant as the people of the Creator of creators (YHWH). Faith that works by love is the motivation that is our call and safe haven. So be it Lord YHWH!

Abbot David Michael

Chapter 17: Washington's Vision at Valley Forge

George Washington had a vision of the emergence of a new nation that was birthed from wars on American soil. I include it here because it does present an indication of the New America as a Union (united people) with a King who will rule over the Republic.

> "I do not know whether it is owing to the anxiety of my mind, or what, but this afternoon, as I was sitting at this table engaged in preparing a dispatch, something seemed to disturb me. Looking up, I beheld standing opposite me a singularly beautiful female. So astonished was I, for I had given strict orders not to be disturbed, that it was some moments before I found language to inquire into the cause of her presence.
>
> A second, a third, and even a fourth time did I repeat my question, but received no answer from my mysterious visitor except a slight raising of her eyes. By this time I felt strange sentiments spreading through me. I would have risen, but the riveted gaze of the being before me rendered volition impossible.
>
> I assayed once more to address her, but my tongue had become useless, even thought itself had become paralyzed. A new influence, mysterious, potent, irresistible, took possession of me.
> All I could do was to gaze steadily, vacantly at my unknown visitor.

Gradually, the surrounding atmosphere seemed as though becoming filled with sensations and luminous. Everything about me seemed to rarify, the mysterious visitor herself becoming more airy, and yet more distinct to my sight than before. I now began to feel as one dying, or rather to experience the sensations which I have sometimes imagined accompany dissolution. I did not think, I did not reason, I did not move; all were alike impossible. I was only conscious of gazing fixedly, vacantly at my companion.

Revolutionary War

"Presently I heard a voice saying, 'Son of the Republic, look and learn,' while at the same time my visitor extended her arm eastwardly. I now beheld a heavy white vapor at some distance rising fold upon fold. This gradually dissipated, and I looked upon a strange scene. Before me lay spread out in one vast plain all the countries of the world -- Europe, Asia, Africa, and America. I saw rolling and tossing between Europe and America the billows of the Atlantic, and between Asia and America lay the Pacific. 'Son of the Republic,' said the same mysterious voice as before, 'look and learn.'

"At that moment I beheld a dark, shadowy being, like an angel floating in mid-air, between Europe and America, dipping water out of the ocean in the hollow of each hand. He sprinkled some upon America with his right hand, while with his left hand he cast some on Europe.

Immediately a dark cloud raised from these countries and joined in mid-ocean. For a while it remained stationary, and then moved slowly westward, until it enveloped America in its murky folds. Sharp flashes of lightning passed through it at intervals, and I heard the smothered groans and cries of the American people."

"A second time the angel dipped water from the ocean, and sprinkled it out as before. The dark cloud was then drawn back to the ocean, in whose heaving billows it sank from view. A third time I heard the mysterious voice saying, 'Son of the Republic, look and learn.' I cast my eyes upon America and beheld villages and towns and cities springing up one after another until the whole land from the Atlantic to the Pacific was dotted with them. Again I heard the mysterious voice say, 'Son of the Republic, the end of the century cometh, look and learn.'

Civil War

"At this the dark, shadowy angel turned his face southward, and from Africa I saw an ill-omened spectre approach our land. It flitted slowly over every town and city. The inhabitants presently set themselves in battle array against each other.

As I continued looking, I saw a bright angel, on whose brow rested a crown of light, on which was traced the word "Union," bearing the American flag, which he placed between the divided nation, and said, 'Remember ye are brethren.' Instantly the inhabitants, casting from them their weapons, became friends once more and united around the National Standard.

"And again I heard the mysterious voice saying, 'Son of the Republic, look and learn.' At this the dark, shadowy angel placed a trumpet to his mouth and blew three distinct blasts; and taking water from the ocean, he sprinkled it upon Europe, Asia, and Africa."

Third War in America

Then my eyes beheld a fearful scene: from each of these countries arose thick, black clouds that were joined into one. And throughout this mass there gleamed a dark red light by which I saw hordes of armed men, who, moving with the cloud, marched by land and sailed by sea to America, which country was enveloped in the volume of the cloud. And I dimly saw these vast armies devastate the whole country and burn the villages, towns, and cities that I beheld were springing up.

As my ears listened to the thundering of the cannon, clashing of swords, and the shouts and cries of millions in mortal combat, I heard again the mysterious voice saying, 'Son of the Republic, look and learn.'

When the voice had ceased, the dark, shadowy angel placed his trumpet once more to his mouth and blew a long and fearful blast."

Darkness Overcome

"Instantly a light as of a thousand suns shone down from above me, and pierced and broke into fragments the dark cloud which enveloped America. At the same moment the angel, upon whose head still shone the word "Union," and who bore our national flag in one hand and a sword in the other, descended from the heavens, attended by legions of white spirits.

These immediately joined the inhabitants of America, who I perceived were well-nigh overcome, but who immediately taking courage again, closed up their broken ranks and renewed the battle.   Again, amid the fearful noise of the conflict, I heard the mysterious voice saying, 'Son of the Republic, look and learn.'

As the voice ceased, the shadowy angel for the last time dipped water from the ocean and sprinkled it upon America. Instantly the dark cloud rolled back, together with the armies it had brought, leaving the inhabitants of the land victorious.

"Then once more I beheld the villages, towns, and cities springing up where I had seen them before, while the bright angel, planting the **azure [blue] standard** he had brought in the midst of them, cried with a loud voice, 'While the stars remain, and the heavens send down dew upon the earth, so long shall the Union last.' And taking from his brow the **crown on which was blazoned the word "Union," he placed it upon the Standard**, while the people, kneeling down, said, 'Amen.'

"The scene instantly began to fade and dissolve, and I at last saw nothing but the rising, curling vapor I at first beheld. This also disappearing, I found myself once more gazing upon the mysterious visitor, who, in the same voice I had heard before, said, 'Son of the Republic, what you have seen is thus interpreted: Three great perils will come upon the Republic. <u>The most fearful is the third</u>, passing which the whole world united shall not prevail against her. Let every child of the Republic learn to live for his God, his land, and the Union.' With these words the vision vanished, and I started from my seat, and felt that I had seen a vision wherein had been shown me the birth, progress, and destiny of the United States."

"Such, my friends," concluded the venerable narrator, "were the words I heard from General Washington's own lips, and America will do well to profit by them."

Abbot David Michael

Analysis

This vision given to George Washington at Valley Forge reveals much about the future of America and the rise of this 6th Kingdom.

Son of the Republic is the tell-tale description of a God created America. Sadly today we can best describe the so-called Union as a declining socialistic democracy controlled by special interest oligopolies.

The term <u>Union in this context does not refer to the North</u> in its unconstitutional aggression against the South but it is the Union as it was founded from the beginning under the protection of YHWH.

The return to a Constitutional Republic is argued by some to be necessary for America to survive but this cannot happen until after a internationally combined invasion of foreign troops under the UN flag occurs on American soil. May U.S. citizens (not real Americans) will side with the enemy against their brothers causing mass destruction across America. The enemy is among us and has hijacked our legal and political government. Only a war against these terrorists running our current government will bring true America back into its Constitutional liberties.

The fact George Washington saw a shield of blue with crown and the name Union on the crown suggests by the crown to be more of a monarchy and not a free republic as emerging from the former United States system. In this we may see a concept of a Monarchical Republic with the people having representation in government as the final YHWH backed United States. As this occurs in joining together the Native Americans with the newer races to the land, we will see peace that may carry into the 1000 year rule and reign of Y'Shua as King upon the earth.

If you are sitting on the fence in this developing conflict, you will be swept up among the passive millions in America who will live in fear and turn against their neighbors for the promise of food, comfort and the illusion of security.

Two Horned [headed] Beast

During this time of the third war in America, the Federalist government in alliance with the foreign UN NWO invaders will also deploy American troops overseas to force the rest of the world to worship the image of the two-horned beast and submit to the power of the Holy Roman Empire.

The Federalists in Washington DC are not Americans but the servants of the Illuminati, the 7 ruling Merovingian Kings and the Jesuit controlled Roman Church. Only as true Americans under YHWH can we resist with the aid of angels and aliens who are in alliance with YHWH.

America will be saved and preserved as the Union of God's people in the West under the guidance of the Melkizedek priesthood. This is a kind of second Israel. America is meant to become a 2nd Jerusalem associated with Davidic ruled Israel with the covenant of the land placed under the protection of the Order of Melkizedek. This sister city of Jerusalem in the West may center in the four corners area of America somewhere stretching down among the ancient city ruins of the mysterious Anasazi people.

Chapter 18: Dream- Feed the Children
Given to John Paul Hennessy on the 26th of January, 2014.

The dream to follow was completely visual, there was no sound, only pictures and feelings. I am not interpreting the dream only reporting what I saw and felt during the dream.

The Dream

I saw you [David] standing alone. I felt you were encamped somewhere near Eureka Springs. Next I saw a group of children between the ages of 5 and 12 as if they they were in a distant land – at least far away from Eureka Springs. The children were wearing uniforms such as common with school children. I believe the uniforms were black and white in color.

The children were all facing you. It became evident they could not see you because you were too far away to be seen but they knew where you were. They seemed to sense your direction and together were facing your direction.

Each child who was facing you was holding an empty white dinner plate. Their faces were without any expression. I could not identify the racial features but they were not white or Caucasian children. Their faces just stared toward you [David] emotionless and fixed.

Then the children were seen to stretch out their arms and held there empty plates out towards you with both hands standing motionless - just waiting. It seemed as though they were beckoning to you to fill their plates. As I watched, their plates suddenly flew from their hands to you to be filled.

Thoughts

This is the most recent of the Native American related dreams.

Although the race of the children in the dram is not clear, it is evident they were not white and not black but of brown skin.

With all of the other evidence suggesting a mission to the Native American, it seems these were Native American children.

The food is not just literal food but also spiritual. We are currently wanting to provide a soup kitchen to move onto a Native Rez in Arizona to fulfill this dream. More can be seen at culdee.net with links to this mission.

Final Thoughts

I am pleased you have taken the time to read this small book. I must confess I am way out of my league in all this and just make a commitment daily to put one foot in front of the other as I am led by the Holy Spirit of YHWH. I am excited about the emergence of the Sisters of the Dove and what it will mean for humanity and its protection from the evil plans of the New World Order powers.

If any reader has any further insight to what is unfolding before us, please send it to me electronically through our publisher.

Blessings

Abbot David Michael, ThD

**FIND MORE BOOKS BY
ABBOT DAVID MICHAEL
AT:**

**info@glentivar.org
http://glentivar.org**

If you want to order 10 copies or more, we can work out a discount for you. +David

www.ingramcontent.com/pod-product-compliance
Lightning Source LLC
Chambersburg PA
CBHW071712040426
42446CB00011B/2037